How to
ACQUIRE
CLIENTS

How to
ACQUIRE
CLIENTS

Powerful Techniques
for the Successful Practitioner

ALAN WEISS, Ph.D.
Author, *The Ultimate Consultant*

JOSSEY-BASS/PFEIFFER
A Wiley Company
www.pfeiffer.com

The ULTIMATE
CONSULTANT
Series

Published by

JOSSEY-BASS/PFEIFFER

A Wiley Company
989 Market Street
San Francisco, CA 94103-1741
415.433.1740; Fax 415.433.0499
800.274.4434; Fax 800.569.0443

www.pfeiffer.com

Jossey-Bass/Pfeiffer is a registered trademark of Jossey-Bass Inc., A Wiley Company.

ISBN: 0-7879-5514-0

Library of Congress Cataloging-in-Publication Data
Weiss, Alan, date
    How to acquire clients : powerful techniques for the successful
practitioner / Alan Weiss.
        p. cm.—(The ultimate consultant series)
Includes index.
    ISBN 0-7879-5514-0 (alk. paper)
    1. Business consultants. 2. Relationship marketing. I. Title.
II. Series.
    HD69.C6 W4593 2002
    001'.068'8—dc21   2001006853

Copyright © 2002 by Alan Weiss

We at Jossey-Bass strive to use the most environmentally sensitive paper stocks available to us. Our
publications are printed on acid-free recycled stock whenever possible, and our paper always meets
or exceeds minimum GPO and EPA requirements.

Acquiring Editor: Matt Davis
Director of Development: Kathleen Dolan Davies
Development Editor: Leslie Stephen
Editor: Rebecca Taff
Senior Production Editor: Dawn Kilgore
Manufacturing Supervisor: Becky Carreño
Interior Design: Gene Crofts
Illustrations: Lotus Art

Printing 10 9 8 7 6 5 4 3 2 1

For my very first client once I opened my doors: GTE.
They called the first morning while I was still figuring out
what I was supposed to be doing,
and I had made $2,500 before lunch.
"You know," I told my wife, "I should have done this a long time ago."
Oh, if it were always so easy!

To L.T. Weiss, always a hero.

Other Works by ALAN WEISS

Books

The Ultimate Consultant Series:

Value-Based Fees: How to Charge—and Get—What You're Worth (2002)
How to Establish a Unique Brand in the Consulting Profession (2001)
The Ultimate Consultant (2001)

How to Sell New Business and Expand Existing Business in Professional Service Firms (2001)
Getting Started in Consulting (2000)
The Unofficial Guide to Power Management (2000)
How to Market, Establish a Brand, and Sell Professional Services (2000)
Good Enough Isn't Enough (1999)
How to Write a Proposal That's Accepted Every Time (1999)
Money Talks (1998)
Million Dollar Consulting (1992; rev. ed. 1998, 2002)
Our Emperors Have No Clothes (1995)
Best Laid Plans (1991)
Managing for Peak Performance (1990)
The Innovation Formula (with Mike Robert, 1988)

Booklets

How to Maximize Fees
Raising the Bar
Leadership Every Day
Doing Well by Doing Right
Rejoicing in Diversity

Audiocassettes

Peak Performance
The Consultant's Treasury
The Odd Couple®

Videos

Stories I Could Never Tell: Alan Weiss Live and Uncensored
Alan Weiss on Marketing
Alan Weiss on Product Development

Newsletters

Balancing Act: Blending Life, Work, and Relationships (electronic)
The Consultant's Craft
What's Working in Consulting (editor)

About the Author

Alan Weiss began his own consulting firm, Summit Consulting Group, Inc., out of his home in 1985 after being fired by a boss with whom he shared a mutual antipathy. Today, he still works out of his home, having traveled to fifty-one countries and forty-nine states, published fifteen books and over four hundred articles, and consulted with some of the great organizations in the world, developing a seven-figure practice in the process.

His clients have included Merck, Hewlett-Packard, Federal Reserve Bank, State Street Corp., Fleet Bank, Coldwell Banker, Merrill Lynch, American Press Institute, Chase, Mercedes-Benz, GE, American Institute of Architects, Arthur Andersen, and over two hundred similar organizations. He delivers fifty keynote speeches a year and is one of the stars of the lecture circuit. He appears frequently in the media to discuss issues pertaining to productivity and performance and has been featured in teleconferences, video conferences, and Internet conferences.

His Ph.D. is in organizational psychology, and he has served as a visiting faculty member at Case Western Reserve, St. John's, and half a dozen other major universities. He currently holds an appointment as adjunct professor at the graduate school of business at the University of Rhode Island, where he teaches a highly popular course on advanced consulting skills. His books have been translated into German, Italian, and Chinese.

The New York Post has called him "one of the most highly regarded independent consultants in the country," and *Success Magazine,* in an editorial devoted to his work, cited him as "a worldwide expert in executive education."

Dr. Weiss resides with his wife of thirty-three years, Maria, in East Greenwich, RI.

Contents

Introduction

Why write a book on business acquisition for highly successful consultants (the primary audience
of *The Ultimate Consultant Series*)? Aren't these the very people
who *have* been acquiring business quite well, thank you very
much?

What I've found is that successful consultants fall victim to
"the success trap." After a while they enter a state of "unconscious competency" in which business flows in, but for reasons
that are long forgotten (and from marketing plans long left stag-
nant due to contemporary success). The success trap is, in reality, a plateau that is rather insidious. The consultant believes that
the journey is still great, and even easier than ever, but that's
because the climb is no longer "up" but rather merely horizon-
tal. And, sooner or later, the laws of entropy obtain and the
plateau erodes into a decline.

I've written this particular book in *The Ultimate Consultant
Series* to help refresh, revitalize, and reawaken successful consultants to the need to continually climb after more and better
business. (And if you're a newer consultant who's decided to
read this book to "jump start" sales, good for you and welcome
aboard!) When I say "better business" I also mean that higher
quality that should accrue to successful people who have paid
the dues and taken the risks: higher fees for less labor-intensive

work; passive income; alliances that drive your business; and selective and appealing instances and locales that combine personal goals with business improvement.

To diversify the offering and guarantee that my "model" isn't the only one presented, I've included four additional elements in every chapter, three of which are contributed by other successful practitioners: "Best Practices" shares highly successful techniques; "The One That Got Away" offers insights gained from failure and, I think, generated a fair degree of commiseration; "The Twilight Zone" demonstrates the unlikely and unimaginable in client acquisition; and my own offering, "Who Could Make This Up?," provides some of the ironies and peculiarities of the wonderful but odd profession we're all a part of.

Read, enjoy, and head up the mountain for better and better sales. It's a great journey. I'll see you up there.

Alan Weiss, Ph.D.
East Greenwich, RI
March 2002

Acknowledgements

My appreciation to Ben Tregoe, who allowed me to make my errors on his nickel and learn my craft on his genius.

CHAPTER 1

Identifying Targets of Opportunity

You Seldom Awake in the Morning with People Waving Money in Your Face

There comes a time in every consultant's career when there is a need to identify and pursue new business and then wrestle it to the ground. Often, that occurs soon after the consultant has hung out a shingle and printed stationery. But, surprisingly, it often occurs only after several years when a highly successful consultant—by repute, contacts, and original momentum—has exhausted that fuel.

In fact, one of the primary reasons for the plateaus and even declines that haunt once-successful practices is that the consultant has never learned to acquire business, because it's always presented itself at the door. I've met people seeking to enter my mentor program, for example, with several years of success and mid-six-figure personal income, whose "marketing materials" are either non-existent or outright embarrassing. They've simply never had the need to sell.

Until next month's mortgage payment begins to loom. By then, it's somewhat late to hit the street.

Selling is a noble profession. It began at the time that technology enabled previously subsistence farmers—virtually everyone alive—to produce more than they could consume. At that moment they had a product to barter with those who weren't such good farmers but had other talents, such as tool repair, music, or weaving. With the advent of currency, items could be sold for a commonly recognized instrument, which itself could be bartered in the future.

In this profession, we are bartering our talent to improve the client's condition. Thus, we'd better learn who the people are who have the shekels that will enable us to barter with the bank at a later time.

THREE CONDITIONS ESSENTIAL TO SUCCESSFUL SELLING

We don't sell in a vacuum. Indeed, we sell in a cross-current of dynamics that strongly influence who will buy and under what conditions. "The race is not always to the swift nor the battle to the strong," observed writer and wit Damon Runyon, "but that's the way to bet." So how do we control, direct, and cajole those forces which, in turn, drive sales?

> The easiest sales take place in an atmosphere of need. The toughest sales occur when the buyer doesn't perceive a need. Consequently, it's better to try to sell people something they perceive will help them, not you.

The highest quality and highest velocity sales I've seen occur at the confluence of three dynamics, as shown in Figure 1.1.

Market Need. This is the existing presence of desire for your services, or the creation of that desire through your marketing endeavors.[1] It means that some buyer wants to achieve a condition which can, one hopes, be filled by your

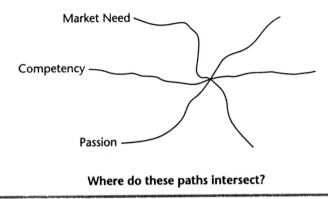

Market Need

Competency

Passion

Where do these paths intersect?

Figure 1.1. Convergence of Need, Competency, and Passion

wares. People enter a McDonald's with the intent of buying food, not to browse. They pull into a gas station to fill the tank, not to bicker about price. (Increasingly, you can pull into a gas station and buy bread and coffee, which is a reflection of catering to additional need through an existing method of distribution.)

In consulting, there should ideally be a need for help in the flavors you offer. When major organizations have strategic needs, many automatically call McKinsey, just as purchasing managers with word processing needs called IBM twenty years ago.

Walt Disney created his own market by inventing the theme park, which no one had been seeking or even thinking about prior to that. In consulting, need is created all the time, as organizations are informed, injected, and overwhelmed with issues, which include diversity, shareholder value, globalization, retaining talent in low unemployment economies, workplace aggression, substance abuse, computer hacking, and so on.

Not many companies were aware of the need for ergonomically sound work stations until several lawsuits created an acute need. Now there are

1. My rule of thumb is that marketing is the creation of need among buyers, and sales is the meeting of that need through the seller's particular alternatives. For marketing steps and plans, see my book, *How to Market, Establish a Brand, and Sell Professional Services* (Fitzwilliam, NH: Kennedy Information, 2000).

legions of consultants working on design and usage of everything from chairs to keyboards.

Note that there may be plenty of need out there, but that your competencies might not match up with them.

There's this wonderful thing about competence. It's not given to you in the manner that brown eyes or allergies are. You can constantly develop competencies, provided that you haven't lost the talent by relying on past successes for future business.

Consultant Competency. I can't fill the need to create more ergonomically sound workplaces because I don't have the skills and am not at all interested in acquiring them. Similarly, I can't meet the needs of clients who have balance sheet issues or technology problems. But I can improve my clients' condition in the areas of performance and leadership, for example, not because I was born with those innate skills, but because I gained them experientially and academically.[2]

Some of us are naturally good listeners or questioners. Some consulting methodology is simple to learn—focus group facilitation comes to mind. But while some people may be "natural" executive coaches, other have to learn the skills more methodically and gain mastery more systematically.

I advise new consultants to begin with what they're already good at, but to constantly learn new skills and acquire new competencies. But what about highly successful consultants who seek to gain new levels? They may have a somewhat tougher job in "unlearning" some of the skills that brought them to where they are in order to move on to the more sophisticated (or timely) skills needed in the future. For example, personality profiling ebbs and flows (although I wish it would permanently ebb), but 360° feedback seems to be a competency that fills

---

2. An interesting issue about consulting competencies is that virtually no one goes to school to be a consultant. Most of us who are solo practitioners are refugees from large companies, meaning that we had better learn the requisite competencies somewhere along the way.

more consistent needs. "Diversity training" will eventually run its course, but selling in a globally connected marketplace will be required for another decade.

When is the last time you brought new skills to your prospects, or to your existing clients? If you're hiring people, are you acquiring new skills or simply replicating those you already have? Is that a wise investment?

The One That Got Away

I've lost three major deals in the past six months, and all for the same reason. I should write on the blackboard five hundred times: "I will not quote a fee for any project to anyone other than the economic buyer." (And then only after establishing some sort of relationship.)

—David Hamacher, President, Communicon Consulting Group, Inc.

Passion. By this stage, you should know that you don't grow by finding something that may make a lot of money and trying to love it. Rather, you find something you love and throw yourself into it. George Merck, one of the founders and leaders of the highly respected pharmaceutical company, observed, "Do good and good will follow." He meant that if your intent is to help your customer, and you become adept at doing that and truly love doing that, you'll never fail to make a profit. Growing at an annual compound rate of over 20 percent for most of its recent history, Merck the company has proved Merck the prophet to be correct.

In Figure 1.2 we see three "typical" consulting trajectories.

Burnout. This is the newcomer to the business who is wildly passionate about the profession and his or her ability to help others. However, because this person quickly runs out of contacts, can't create new need, and doesn't really have unique and/or effective competencies, there is a relatively rapid decline. The "burnout" rate for such people is very high and very abrupt, since they're running on blind passion. They have ignored need and competence. These are often the people with a single "message" or methodology, who feel that mere intensity alone can create need in others. It can't.

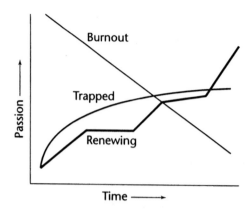

Figure 1.2. Three Trajectories of Consultants' Passion

Trapped. This is the profile of the more methodical consultants, who build a practice and become quite successful. Their passion climbs steadily until, subliminally and unperceived at the time, their ardor cools. Some retire early, others think of some way to try to sell their practice. Most continue to "go through the motions," but don't understand why the work isn't as much fun and the business isn't growing as it once did. I often refer to this as "the success trap." Consultants here are going through the motions, but are no longer enraptured by what they do, because they can do it in their sleep. They have, consciously or unconsciously, stopped developing their abilities and ceased acquiring new competencies.[3]

Passion means that you are excited about what you do. You rejoice in the highs; you don't wallow in the lows. Passion is about being energized, being "psyched," being ready to go full-throttle every time. If that doesn't sound familiar, then you may well be in "the success trap."

Renewing. This is the constantly renewing consultant. This individual grows, takes some breathing room while success is absorbed and business is

---

3. When a solo practitioner seeks to grow the practice through the hiring of professionals and does not use that opportunity to acquire new competencies in those new hires (but merely hires mirror images of his or her own competencies, which could just as easily be subcontracted for by the day), I'm perplexed. Physician heal thyself.

solidified, *but then becomes passionate again about new clients, new markets, new skills, and new environments.* The ultimate consultant is one who is constantly self-renewing, periodically re-energized, and continually thrilled about the nature of the work.

Your initial targets of opportunity to acquire new clients—no matter what the stage of your career—will be found at the confluence of market need, competence to meet that need, and passion for that competence. The bad news is that too few veteran consultants step back to admire that view. The good news is that all three dynamics, and hence the keys to new business acquisition, are within our own influence.

GENERALIZING AND SPECIALIZING: THE VIEW FROM CONTRARIAN LAND

There has been a rubric in our business about the need to "specialize or die," which sounds to me an awful lot like New Hampshire's license plate motto.[4]

One can make a case for specializing early in one's career, when focus, a more limited skill set, the need for a quick "brand" in the marketplace, and other competitive factors mitigate against attempting to throw too wide a net into the ocean. But I don't think that's where ultimate consultants belong. In fact, I can make a case that generalization is where you thrive, while specialization allows you merely to survive.

The acquisition of new business is greatly enhanced when the number of potential clients (the breadth of the marketplace need you can meet with your competencies) is maximized. For example, the two "walls" that provide boundaries to my practice were those cited above: I don't do financial or technological work. But anything—and I mean anything—in the realm of individual and organizational performance between those walls is fair game for

---

4. Actually, a very charming and talented woman named Juanell Teague in Texas has made "specialize or die" her imprimatur in coaching consultants. I disagree with her most respectfully. (The New Hampshire license plates actually read "Live Free or Die," which is close enough.)

Back in my computer technology days, I wrote an article on contingency planning and posted it on our website. The article explained every single thing you would need to do to prepare a working contingency plan that would keep you in business in the event of a lengthy computer system shutdown. (Literally anyone with half a brain could read the article and create his or her own plan.)

In addition to the article, we created a database system that could be used to gather and store all the information needed to make the plan work. Both the article and the database system were given away for free from our website.

I didn't track how many times the article was read, but it was reprinted about thirty times in newspapers, magazines, and newsletters around the world, and the database was downloaded by 6,300 different businesses during an eighteen-month period.

On the surface you'd think I was nuts for giving away something so popular. However, I wasn't in the business of creating and selling software systems. I was in the business of managing projects. By giving away the article and database for free, I created the credibility I needed to book our calendar with contingency planning projects. And the really interesting part is the extremely short sales process that resulted. You see, since people who contacted me had already read the article, they knew exactly what they were getting if they hired me. So the only thing left to discuss was price and availability (I was closing $80,000 engagements in fifteen-minute phone conversations).

Now that I've switched to sales and marketing consulting as my career, I've extended this to include a free one-hour workshop each month. I call it the Honest Selling Breakfast Club and almost all of the business I've gotten this past year has come as a result of giving people free access to this information.

If you give it, they will pay you for it.

—Gill E. Wagner, President, Honest Selling

Who Could Make This Up?

I called on the senior vice president for human resources at a huge media company headquartered in New York. He told me that his staff had significant needs and that they needed to be transformed into powerful internal consultants.

He had several of his staff in the room and played to the grandstand. He explained that he was going to make major inroads in changing the organizations and the thinking of management. He wanted "world class" and the "best of the best." During all this pontification, I noticed some furtive looks from his staff and what seemed like utter boredom from his administrative assistant, who had set the meeting up for us.

At his insistence, I sent him a proposal by FedEx based on the objectives and metrics he provided during our session. When I hadn't heard anything in three days, I called him and persevered until I got him on the phone. He told me my proposal was so out of the ballpark, so ridiculous, that it had actually upset his stomach. The proposal, to help with his inroads and change, was a mere $27,000. (I've never met a human resource executive who could spend freely from his or her own budget, so I kept this modest in order to break into the organization.) He told me that he would "go in another direction."

I sent down, via FedEx, a pack of Pepto-Bismol™ tablets so that his stomach could recover. Of course, for maximum exposure, I sent them with my note to his administrative assistant.

—AW

me. I have engaged in a strategy of trying to create the broadest possible range of prospects. I'd rather deselect those who aren't right for me than have the prospect deselect me on the basis of too narrow a specialty.[5]

When you have come as far in your career as the reader of this book presumably has, there should be a tropism at work forcing more of a generalist view, despite the specialties that may have been responsible for getting you where you are. Those influences include both the obvious and the subtle.

Factors Supporting Moves Toward Generalist Positions

A veteran consultant's experiential base has become significant, and the nature and breadth of assignments will have inevitably created the basis for appealing to wider needs with increasing competencies.

One's name and/or "brand" has developed to the point that credibility is attached to your repute, not solely earned through future projects. Buyers will trust your ability to do what you say you can do.

Relationship skills will have been developed to the point where trust is formed with key buyers early rather than late. The veteran has heard all the objections there are to hear and is prepared to deal with them smoothly (or shame on the consultant).

One probably has acquired additional resources—subcontractors, employees, alliance partners—that provide additional competencies and abilities at the disposal of the consultant.

The nature of client concerns, the economy, the environment, and social conditions have continued to change and evolve, so that the consultant, while not abandoning original skills, has at least had to modify and develop them to stay abreast of need over the long term.

There's simply more challenge and fun in trying new things and learning new skills, and the successful consultant has more confidence and resilien-

---

5. I maintain a resource list of consulting help for projects that aren't suited for me or that don't interest me at this point in my career. It just knocks me out when one of the applicants lists a specialty such as "telemarketing for medium-size mortgage lenders," rather than simply "telemarketing" or even just "sales." It's sort of like a manicurist who is willing to deal only with the ring finger on the left hand. Not much need for that.

cy (toleration of failure) than a less experienced person. I've heard a great many consultants, about to try something new, say, "What's the worst that can happen? There is no boss to fire me!"

Specialization is a weak cop-out for the new consultant and is a cardinal sin for the successful consultant. It's simply crazy to learn more and more about less and less, especially when new technologies, larger competitors, or a fickle clientele (remember outdoor experiences and left brain/right brain thinking?) can pull the narrow rug out from under the specialist. Generalists tend to have wall-to-wall carpeting.

At any stage in one's career, whether neophyte or veteran, struggler or impresario, there is a constant need to refresh the practice with new business. The dynamics you can quickly and effectively manipulate are the needs of the market, your competencies to meet them, and your passion to undertake the initiatives. If that's the "arrow," then the size of the target is determined by how much of a generalist you decide—emphasis on the phrase *you decide*—to become.

If your target is tiny, represented by a highly specialized skill aimed at a narrow range of prospects, then your aim has to be precise and you have to hit the target before other marksmen—both the competing specialists *and* the generalists who also embrace that need—hit it before you do. However, if your target is much wider and more general, not only do the demands on your accuracy decline, but you'll also find targets of opportunity abounding, many of which have few if any competitors shooting at the same mark.

There should be a natural movement toward a more generalist position as your career progresses and thrives. Don't dampen it; encourage it. Your ability to attract new business and new clients will be directly proportional to your ability to position yourself as most appealing to most people. In other words, you don't want to be the equivalent of William Tell.

CUSTOMIZED ASSAULTS: WHEN THERE IS A SINGLE TARGET TOO APPEALING TO RESIST

The stereotypical "target of opportunity" is an organization the needs of which represent a particular match for your competencies and passion. We see this with executives—Gordon Bethune was the perfect leader to turn around Continental Airlines because he refocused on performance and not the marketplace fads—and the same holds true for consultants.

> There is never a good excuse to "cold call," no matter how tempting a client, because that's not how buyers tend to buy. However, there are excellent ways to turn a "cold" call into a tepid or even warm call, if you take the time to plan an attack on the highest priority targets.

Pursuing a target "cold" is difficult for the best of us, no matter how strong our brand or deep our experience. But when the "call of the prospect" is overwhelming, and you don't have a particular "in" or introduction to a buyer, there are some criteria to use to determine whether a customized "assault" on this target makes economic sense.

Ten Criteria to Test "Cold Call" Viability

1. Do you have strong experience in the target's industry?
2. Do you have strong experience with the type of issues the target is grappling with?
3. Can you cite a third party the client respects who can validate your work?
4. Can you visit the target economically (target is in your area, or you can easily be in his or her area, since multiple visits will probably be necessary)?
5. Can you reach and influence people who can help pave the way, for example, trade association executives, vendors, customers, and so forth?

6. Can you arrange to speak in front of key managers from that company at some common, external event?
7. Can you publish something in the trade press or a specialized publication which key managers are likely to read or be familiar with?
8. Is there a function you can attend that will enable you to meet managers from the target in an informal and casual setting?
9. Can you use the Internet to find some detailed information that will help you tailor an approach specifically for your target?
10. Do you have the courage and perseverance to pursue this target, even in the face of multiple rejections?

If you can muster at least five affirmatives to my list, then you have a decent probability of at least reaching a significant buyer and moving toward a proposal. If you can honestly generate six to eight "yeses," then this should be a high priority target for you. (If you can answer positively to nine or all ten questions, then this is a better prospect than many where you already know the buyer!)

For newer consultants, where most people make the case that lack of a client base and lack of a "name" make cold calling the default strategy, there is more of a need to target than ever. Most newer people waste their time on scattered, generic, and blanket marketing approaches. (And I can make a case that newer consultants should invest more energy in drawing people to them than in trying to beat doors down.)

For successful consultants with strong track records, creating these targets of opportunity make more sense. There is an experiential base to build on, a certain "brand" recognition to parlay, and the sheer bravado necessary that develops after both a gazillion rejections *and* hundreds or thousands of acceptances along the path to success.

One of the factors impeding people from "ultimate consulting" is that they tend to ride their successes and gradually eschew—often subconsciously—the risk taking and uncertainties that they once aggressively entertained. When you are solely accepting business based on the path of least resistance (name recognition, word of mouth, client referral, and so on) you will, inevitably, wind up in a rut that may result in my "success trap." The time to experiment, accept prudent risk, and "test the envelope" is when you're successful and dealing from a position of strength.

> If you are doing very well and never failing, then you are not suffi-
> ciently trying to broaden your scope, or failing and not realizing it, or
> lying. The time to take risks is when you're successful. Otherwise, the
> power of success is muted and it becomes mundane. When you're
> successful, you can afford more risk—going after totally new cus-
> tomers and markets—because you're gambling with "house money."

For the successful consultant, creating these specific "targets of opportunity" might not be the way to make a living day in and day out, but the technique
is very useful in bringing new and diverse clients into the fold on a regular
basis. Even the best of clients eventually disappear, and we all need the life
blood. Over a twelve-year period, I must have completed thirty-five or forty
projects for Merck around the world, worth perhaps nearly $2,000,000 in
income for me. Then it all simply stopped. Key projects were successfully fin-
ished, important buyers retired, top leadership changed, and a combination of
normal events locked me out.

Fortunately, I had also used that decade to build a solid business in a variety of industries, frequently using Merck as part of my credibility, and using
wonderful people at Merck as references. If I had allowed myself to become a
"one trick pony," you wouldn't be reading this book right now!

STRATEGIES FOR ISOLATING AND HITTING NEW TARGETS OF OPPORTUNITY

Using the guidelines above, here is a brief example of how you might leverage each factor (though unreasonable, perhaps, and unnecessary, I wanted to
make sure we covered each one) for a hypothetical approach to the *New York
Times*.

1. Do you have strong experience in the target's industry?
   You have experience working with the *Hartford Courant*, which is your

sole newspaper client over the years. However, your original buyer is still there and willing to give you a testimonial.[6]

2. Do you have strong experience with the type of issues the target is grappling with?

    You've read that the *Times* is suffering from a dearth of new talent, since their pay scale on the editorial side is low and the competition for talent from a variety of media is intense. Simply working for the *Times* isn't a sufficient inducement any more. You have worked on a similar problem with Hewlett-Packard, wherein the HP name was no longer adequate to harvest the crème de la crème of graduates. Although vastly different organizations, the basic issue is identical.

3. Can you cite a third party the client respects who can validate your work?

    You know an associate director at the American Press Institute, to which the *Times* belongs, who was in college with you.

4. Can you visit them economically (they are in your area, or you can easily be in their area, since multiple visits will probably be necessary)?

    You have clients in New York and are there on business at least twice a month in any case. Adding even a day to the trip is a minor expense.

5. Can you reach and influence people who can help pave the way, for example, trade association executives, vendors, customers, and so forth?

    You did a favor for the business editor of the *Boston Globe*, which is owned by the *Times*, when he needed an interview quickly on a breaking business news story and found your name on the Internet. He might be willing to reciprocate by providing some names and even an introduction.

6. Can you arrange to speak in front of key managers from that company at some common, external event?

    The American Association of Newspaper Publishers conducts meetings around the country every quarter. You can pursue their executive director to find out what it would take to get on the agenda, perhaps using the *Courant* and *Globe* contacts as an introduction.

---

6. One of the chronic mistakes of successful consultants is that they stop asking for testimonials, which are an essential piece of ammunition for any new target.

> If you build an intelligent plan and are willing to persevere, eventually you will reach a key buyer. If you simply throw yourself repeatedly against the side of their headquarters, you will eventually kill yourself.

7. Can you publish something in the trade press or a specialized publication that key managers are likely to read or be familiar with?

   The Inland Press Association, although in another part of the country, has a house organ open to freelancers. You can query the publisher to investigate submitting a piece on attracting talent in highly competitive environments, citing your HP experiences but adapting them for the newspaper industry.

8. Is there a function you can attend that will enable you to meet managers from the target in an informal and casual setting?

   There will be a symposium on "Media and the Electoral Process" held at John Jay College, which is open to the public. There is a cocktail hour before and a question and answer session after the panel discussion.

9. Can you use the Internet to find some detailed information that will help you tailor an approach specifically for your target?

   You've pursued employment opportunities through the *Times'* website, and then through traditional means, and have found key errors in the approach to new hires that you can document and improve readily.

10. Do you have the courage and perseverance to pursue this target, even in the face of multiple rejections?

    You want the *Times* as a client, you have a thriving business, you've gained a great deal of ammunition through the above exercise, and you have nothing to lose.

Before you claim that I've been somewhat overzealous in my optimism about the assault on the *Times*, consider this: Anyone who has been in this business for a few years and enjoying success can develop the kind of resources, initiative, and approaches that I've suggested. The problem isn't one of availability; it's one of volition.

The Twilight Zone

I was competing for an out-of-town consulting assignment, had been interviewed locally by the potential client, and had submitted a proposal. The client called and told me that he had narrowed his choice down to one other consultant and me. He asked me to tell him what I would charge to make a one-day visit to his offices, speak to a few people, and prepare a brief (1- or 2-page) analysis of the situation as I saw it.

My response was to specify an amount that I would charge, but that I would waive it if I was given the consulting assignment. He said that he would get back to me.

When he did, he told me that he would pay me the amount I requested regardless of his ultimate decision. I was given the assignment and am still consulting for this client ten years later.

—Don Steig, CMC, Practical Computer Solutions

FROM MY TIME IN THE TRENCHES

The juncture of market need, professional competency, and personal passion is where brilliant careers are forged and perpetuated. It's vital to understand and embrace the fact that needs can be created, competencies acquired, and passions expanded.

In other words, this dynamic is not a fait accompli, but rather a set of factors you can manage and exploit. One of the royal roads to business acquisition is in finding that confluence for yourself and then constantly expanding it to admit more and more new business territory.

> The creation of new targets of opportunity should be low volume, focused, and highly intense—a rifle shot, not a shotgun. Ironically, the fewer totally new targets you choose to pursue, the higher the likelihood that your focus and intensity will pay off. Less is more.

The generalist will be in a far better position to determine which new business is appropriate and what conditions are acceptable, because the range and scope of potential buyers is so much greater than that of the specialist. The latter has more pressure to accept business under any conditions and is constantly in danger of a specialty that obsolesces or is superceded by a huge competitor. In terms of the trajectory of one's consulting career, the movement should be from specialist to generalist, not the other way around. (And the more quickly you can escape the specialist trap, the better.)

Customized, targeted assaults on particularly high potential prospects are entirely appropriate for veteran consultants, and the simple use of a "targeting checklist" can greatly enhance the odds of success, not by creating new opportunity but by simply reorganizing and redeploying the assets that the consultant has already generated and has in place.

New business acquisition is like fresh air. You can never be content with what's simply in your lungs, and the fresh air of a few moments ago is carbon dioxide now. Stop holding your breath.

CHAPTER 2

How to Prepare for Success in Acquiring New Business

The Allies Didn't Simply Decide to Take a Trip Across the English Channel One Morning

When I first opened my own business in 1983, prior to my current Summit Consulting Group, Inc.— meaning I had stationery printed and incorporated as "AJW Associates"—I arose one morning, showered and shaved, and went into my den to sit near my business phone. I was still there at lunch time, having read the local newspaper, *The Wall Street Journal, Time* magazine, and several other periodicals that had been gathering dust in a corner. (How I got on the list of *Today's Handyman* is still a mystery.)

My wife put up with this for a week and told me that I'd better think of another way to attract business, or get myself another real job. After another week of mulling over that, and running out of all possible reading material, I did pursue a real job, and my current company wasn't born until 1985. Sometimes it's better to be lucky than good, and by that time, having served as CEO of a small consulting firm in the interim, I began to know what I didn't know.

I was such a naïf at the outset of AJW Associates (I only let the incorporation lapse a few years ago because I was so emotionally attached to it) that, when my attorney asked me for three names for the business for incorporation, I gave him my wife's, daughter's, and son's, assuming he needed board members and thankful that I had three other people in the immediate family. My attorney was a very patient man, but I know he was betting that I'd never make it past the first six months. He turned out to be overly optimistic.

I've since learned a lot about the various approaches to acquiring business. I'm going to focus on the best sales techniques here, as opposed to marketing efforts, since I've covered marketing in significant depth elsewhere and because this book is for the development of sales skills in consulting.[1] In the final section of this chapter, however, we will deal with the *results* of successful marketing: What to do when prospects approach you. For now, though, let's look at how to approach them.

> You cannot sell to anyone who doesn't trust you. And no one will trust you who doesn't see you. This is not rocket science. This is selling science 101.

THE FRONTAL ATTACK

The best method to acquire business is through the front door and into a buyer's face. Selling consultative services is a *relationship business*, and, consequently, none of the following works well at all:

---

1. See, for example, *How to Market, Establish a Brand, and Sell Professional Services: From Anonymity to Credibility to Celebrity* (Fitzwilliam, NH: Kennedy Information, 2000) and the earlier books in this series.

Dealing with recommenders, gatekeepers, purchasing agents, subordinates to the buyer, and so on

Selling "features and benefits" of your approach, which will get you quickly relegated to the appropriate subordinate in charge of sales, human resources, or widget repair

Emphasizing your methodology or approach, which is of incredible interest to incredibly few people other than yourself

Talking instead of listening

Definition

Economic Buyer: That person who can write a check without anyone else's approval (that is, who has his or her own budget and discretion) for the value that you are providing. I often call this person the "true buyer."

Veteran consultants have often allowed the "full frontal sales muscle" to atrophy because they've been so successful with word of mouth, a hot book, a huge client who pays all the bills, and other factors. Sometimes those salutary conditions last a career. Usually, they don't.

In a frontal attack, it's vital to have three conditions in place:

1. You know the name of the economic buyer.
2. You have the ability or opportunity to meet that buyer.
3. You have the confidence to interact as a peer.

1. You Know the Name of the Economic Buyer

Economic buyers are not discernable by rank or serial number. They are distinguished by having budget and discretion to spend it on the likes of us. My most important buyer at Merck had the title "manager of international development" and, at Hewlett-Packard, "director of knowledge management." While I've also sold to presidents and every other high-level executive, I've also acquired very lucrative contracts from people whose titles belie their actual clout.

The Twilight Zone

One sale that sticks out is an attempt by a sales rep who was working for me to use the "impending event" technique to close a major sale. She was eight-and-a-half months pregnant at the time. She told the customer, "This is the last sales call I'm going to make before I go on maternity leave, so can I please have the order today?"

She got the order.

—Herb Fox, MultiTrack Sales Consulting

Find the economic buyer, by name and not title, by asking these types of questions of yourself or of knowledgeable people within the target organization.

Ten Questions to Help Identify Economic Buyers
1. Who is responsible for that operation's success?
2. Who establishes and submits the budget for that operation?
3. Who will be held accountable for success or failure?
4. Who has contracted with consultants and hired them previously?
5. To whom do others defer about tough decisions?
6. Who is the court of last resort on allocating budget or transferring budgets?
7. Who has discrete, self-contained projects reliant on no other department?
8. Who has been given budget specifically to support other areas' needs?
9. Who can veto any initiative in this area?
10. Who is setting the priorities in this operation?

Definition

Relationship: A comfort level with an economic buyer wherein each of you respects the other, listens to the other, and feels comfortable disagreeing and "pushing back" in areas of disagreement. There is mutual trust and the belief that you are peers, both considering whether to work collaboratively on a project; there is not a perceived "buyer" and "seller," or "superior" and "subordinate."

How to Acquire Clients

2. You Have the Ability to Meet the Buyer

Once you know who the buyer is, you have to be able to meet him or her. That means that the person is accessible (not in Katmandu), willing to meet (no endless committees and gatekeepers), and not distracted (no ten-minute hurried interviews between "more important" matters).

One of the great benefits of being successful in this business is that you have money to invest in your business. I've always been willing to get on an airplane at my own expense (or at the sacrifice of omnipresent frequent flyer miles) to see a true buyer who represents major potential business for me. In fact, when consultants ask me if they should invest in such business acquisition pursuits, I always tell them to apply the same criteria:

Will you meet the economic buyer?
Does that buyer agree to provide you with at least one hour of uninterrupted time?
Does the buyer agree to the fact that, ideally, you would like to exchange information and share views that will lead to your submitting a proposal?
Is it understood that any consulting work requested—for example, interviewing managers, providing feedback on observations, assessing business protocols, suggesting better techniques, and so on—will be subject to a fee?[2]

Never make a sales call—even if it's across the street—unless you're going to meet with the economic buyer, identify the economic buyer, or meet with someone who can help you get to the economic buyer. If you have any other intent, you're wasting your time.

3. You Have the Confidence to Interact as a Peer

This is the most difficult aspect, and it is violated by veterans as much as it is by neophytes, but for different reasons. New consultants often feel that they don't

---

2. It's vital to separate a sales call from consulting help. You can always "rebate" the fee against the larger project if your proposal is accepted.

have sufficient experience and depth and that they "don't belong" in the same room. They see themselves, often subconsciously, as "impostors" who are lucky to be there and who will soon be discovered and tossed. (Which, of course, becomes a self-fulfilling prophesy.)

Veterans suffer from a different disease. They tend to see their success as based on their approaches, and they've tended to become rather one-dimensional. That is, they can talk (endlessly) about their expertise, but can't talk as fluently (or listen empathically) to the buyer's needs.

The confidence to interact as a peer means that the consultant must be a peer. That includes a wealth of business knowledge, a breadth of general knowledge, a command of the language, a sense of humor, and very highly refined listening skills. (Hard as I've tried, I find I just can't learn anything about someone else when I'm talking.) The greatest relationship pitfall of successful consultants is that they've allowed themselves to become narrow people. Ironically, but understandably, the most successful consultants in selling their services are the ones who are the most well-rounded and complete people, able to "mesh" with a wide variety of buyers in very little "face time."

As I write this, I'm working with an advertising organization that is not achieving the desired results with its external sales force. When I investigated, I found that the entire national sales organization was achieving *fewer than two calls a week with prospects, and I estimated that less than half of those calls were with real economic buyers.* Many readers have encountered similar circumstances (and made a small fortune using such common sense to help the client).

The same paradigm applies to us. If we are not seeing buyers, we are not going to expand our businesses. The easiest, quickest, and least expensive way to do that is to find out who they are, arrange for a meeting, and have the confidence to quickly build a trusting relationship. Otherwise, we're not consultants, but merely the shoeless cobbler's children.

Someone once asked me "Who are your prospective customers?" I responded, "Just about everyone until . . ." "Until what?" "Until I determine whether they are customers or not. That should be my decision, not theirs!"

THE FLANKING MANEUVER

There are times when the economic buyer is just not going to see you. None of the steps above might work, or you might be uncertain (or have made an error) about the identity of the economic buyer.

It's time for a flanking maneuver.

A flanking move is one that moves you closer to the economic buyer in subtle ways, through a side door instead of the front door. This isn't devious and isn't unethical. It's simply a set of smart techniques that will enable you to meet someone whom you really can help if given the opportunity.

Here are some examples of this more indirect approach.

Ten Techniques to Grease the Skids Directly to the Economic Buyer
1. Use a third-party reference to introduce you.
2. Send a book or an article that addresses the buyer's current needs.
3. Send some insights about the industry, the competition, and/or the customers.
4. Meet informally at a trade association or a civic or social event.
5. Speak at a conference attended by the buyer.
6. Publish an article in a publication read by the buyer.
7. Obtain an interview in the buyer's local newspaper.
8. Get the buyer's email address (almost always available from the switchboard) and send a brief, provocative message requesting a phone call or meeting.
9. If distant, inform the buyer you'll "be in town" on certain days. Always provide options. The farther from your home base, the more likely the buyer will agree to meet with you.
10. Shop the buyer's business, develop some insights to improve the operation and/or end major problems, then provide these to the buyer and suggest a more detailed discussion.

Think of a flanking maneuver as the ability to appear on the buyer's "radar screen." Sometimes, multiple appearances are required ("Didn't we meet before?" or "Haven't I read something of yours?" or "Didn't you send me a book?"). Sometimes, a single highly effective appearance is enough ("A good friend of mine mentioned you to me. I'm glad we've met at this convention.").

Flanking maneuvers work best when they get you permanently and repeatedly onto the economic buyer's radar screen. They work worst when you're maneuvering to get the attention of the wrong people.

Committees are virtually never decision makers, no matter what the members claim. (Yes, I know you can recall one or two exceptions, but the fact that you can proves my point about how rare that is.) As experienced consultants, we also all know by now that the following job titles are seldom, if ever, economic buyers:

Training director
Human resource manager
Sales trainer
Purchasing manager
Assistant general counsel
Audit manager
Internal consultant

If we are going to spend time trying to arrange the right steps and sequences—an often elaborate choreography—that lead us to the buyer, then we have to make absolutely sure that no one trips us up along the way. The most powerful approach is to deal with these people and others like them to gain information and to gain access to the true buyer. The worst approach is to become trapped in their indecisive webs, but never go beyond them.

The problem, of course, is that feasibility and lower level people are relatively easy to see, and eager for relationships. They are quite happy to have lunch, spend time on the phone, exchange emails, and engage in the most obtuse details of your methodology and philosophy. But you're better off with

> Even experienced consultants get their priorities wrong. They tend to spend too much time on perfecting their "pitch" and not enough time finding out who controls the checkbook. It's very easy to build solid relationships with the wrong people.

a mediocre relationship with a real economic buyer than with a superb relationship with a feasibility buyer.

Flanking maneuvers should be a standard part of your repertoire, because this is what is accomplished by solid marketing. The more you speak, publish, network, hold breakfasts, lead professional associations, engage in pro bono work, create products, write newsletters, and so forth, the more radar screens you're going to appear on. Almost any referral is a flanking attack, for example.

INFILTRATION

There are times (too many of them) when both frontal assault and flanking maneuvers fail. You are locked out of the castle, or so it seems.

These are times when infiltration may work. Infiltration occurs when you use subtle and non-obvious means to meet the buyer. The Trojan Horse evokes subterfuge and trickery, perhaps, but it did get the job done.

Here are some of the means of infiltration—being invited into the keep virtually unnoticed.

Ten Techniques to Infiltrate Any Organization

1. Become a Customer. If you're really serious about learning the inside workings of a high potential banking prospect, invest some money in the place. If the target is a brokerage, move some investments over there. It didn't hurt me at all with Mercedes when it turned out I was driving a top-of-the-line model and, consequently, was on referral terms with one of their most successful dealership owners. Spend some money, become known to local managers, do something to assist the store. Try to pick an operation that has appeal to you in any case. I didn't mind driving the Mercedes at all, but I would have had a hard time taking up scuba diving. One day, flying first class on Delta, I met their number two ranking officer, sitting across the aisle, testing out customer reaction.

> I'm constantly surprised at how stupid I was just two weeks ago. There are many ways to a buyer's heart. Remember, you're pursuing the quarry because you're able to be of help. You're doing the buyer a favor.

2. Perform Pro Bono Work.   Find out what causes or charities your target supports, and throw yourself into them. In the worst case you'll become known as a supporter, and in the best case you'll find yourself working elbow-to-elbow with the prospect's key officers. Choose something you believe in and you'll be helping the cause, the prospect, and yourself. I made a sale to a police department when I served in a very visible board position alongside the department's chief.

3. Create a "Study" or "White Paper."   Invest some time and money in becoming an "instant authority" by sponsoring or actually conducting a study in that industry. If you want to penetrate an insurance prospect, create a research report on the propensity of consumers to buy from traditional agents versus over the Internet. If you're after the beverage industry, conduct an investigation into the popularity of "sports drinks" versus traditional beverages. These can be anecdotal and not scientific. The key is to create an item and aura of interest to your prospective buyers.

4. Engage in Civic Activities.   You are, after all, a "catch" for the local zoning, planning, waterfront, environmental, port, and school boards. Volunteer your expertise. Serve alongside some potential clients or recommenders. Get your name in the paper as an advocate of some position.

5. Write About Your Prospect.   If you're writing an article, "white paper," column, or book, mention your target in complimentary language. Cite them as a fine example of teamwork, or innovation, or globalization, or diversity. Send copies of your published praise to your intended buyer—who might well have already heard of your kindness through the public relations department and/or clipping services. You might just be invited to address the board or at least tour the operation.

6. Become a Professor.   This is not as far-fetched as it sounds. I've served as visiting professor at Case Western Reserve (for seven years), the University of Illinois, the Graduate School of Business at the University of Georgia, St. John's, and the University of Rhode Island Graduate School of Business (where I hold an adjunct professor's appointment for teaching one evening a week).[3] The professorial duties will enable you to use your target as a class example, project, or research source. (I used Marine Midland Bank, Merck, and Hewlett-Packard in my Ph.D. dissertation research.)

BEST PRACTICES

Sometimes, executives are starry-eyed over the latest buzz words or consulting products, and you have to deal with this effectively. In the mid-90s, I was talking to a senior executive about a potential strategy development assignment. He was obviously into reengineering, which had reached its peak and was actually in decline then. "I'm talking to another major consulting firm about reengineering," he told me, very taken with their comprehensive and step-by-step approach.

"I see," I said softly, adding quietly and a bit sadly, "We used to do reengineering." I purposely didn't say another word. There was silence. "What?" the client stammered. "What do you mean you 'used to do it.' Why did you stop? What happened?"

He was flustered. This unleashed a torrent of questions and emotions, and I redirected the discussion towards the fact that the client's company faced a growth challenge, which reengineering wasn't going to fix. I got the project, needless to say, and he quickly got rid of the other firm with all the fancy reengineering charts.

—Andrew Sobel, Institute for Business Renewal

---

3. Don't worry about your schedule and commitments. A modern college professor has only slightly more power than a medieval satrap.

7. Write an Unabashed Letter of Praise.   Find something your prospect has done well—whether personally, for high quality, or universally, for saving the rain forests—and send your compliments. This also works in praising an employee. (If you want to get an executive's private address, don't tell the assistant that you have a complaint, just mention that you want to send a letter of congratulations and you'll quickly have the person's private email, car phone, and secret decoder ring.)

> Put yourself in the buyer's shoes. What would induce you to want to find out more about someone? Are they citing you, referencing your company, providing alternatives for the position you're in, being provocative about the environment? What constitutes your "Trojan Horse"?

8. Befriend an Employee.   Employees understand their employers. Get to know the bank teller or the supermarket cashier. Spend some time chatting with the retail branch manager. Chat up the ticket agent at the airport that serves as your home base. I once landed an Internet specialty company when an employee at a speech I was making told me their weakness wasn't technology but sales. I wrote to the CEO and enclosed some sales tips for high-tech businesses. He invited me out and we were immediately simpatico.

9. Watch Your Serendipity.   Every day we receive offers, inducements, and appeals that we consign to the wastebasket or simply ignore. But within them—and the few seconds required to consider hidden opportunity—can lie fortunes. A request to submit a free article to a new diversity newsletter resulted in my being published over a dozen times by a thankful, struggling editor. As the publication grew in stature, my largest client realized that I was doing work in diversity and commissioned a new project in that area. I then used that with prospects who had such needs, now able to cite my large client for credibility.

10. Meet the Buyer Socially.   If you're really serious about a major prospect, then join a country club, attend a charitable event, become a member of a trade association, or do whatever it takes to meet that buyer on comfortable, social grounds. It is neither legend nor accident that many deals have been consummated on golf courses. I barely talk to people socially, yet I've closed two deals on an airplane, one with the vice president of marketing of a specialty manufacturer, and one with the president of North American Operations of a major auto manufacturer. Those were accidental meetings. But if you can deliberately arrange to "accidentally" meet these people, you'll be in a strong position. I want to emphasize two things: First, we're talking about major buyers who can make your future rosy; second, we're talking about your ability to truly help these people meet their own personal and professional goals.

The One That Got Away

[My biggest mistake was] giving away the solution in the sales call to a prospect in the first five minutes instead of giving them sufficient proof of the value I would bring in terms of previous experiences I had had in solving similar problems.

I had to learn that my speed in coming up with a solution was not as important as my ability to develop a trusting bond. They got free advice and I got the door.

—Andrew J. Birol, Business Development Expert and President, PACER Associates, Inc.

Frontal attacks, flanking maneuvers, and infiltration—all excellent tactics to reach and convince buyers of your merits. But there is one more dynamic, which seems relatively simple but which consultants at all levels of their careers often mishandle.

When buyers come to you, it is an unparalleled opportunity to maximize the sale. This is not unethical, not immoral, not illegal. This being the case, why would you refrain from doing that?

WHEN THE BUYER COMES TO YOU (BUILD IT, AND THEY WILL COME)

Buyers will sometimes come to you, occasionally out of accident or curiosity, but more often as a result of successful marketing efforts and word of mouth. I want to spend a bit of time on this before we close this chapter.

When clients come to you, it is not a time to rejoice, slap yourself on the back, and cater to the buyer's desires. It is, rather, a time to realize that the buying dynamic is now substantially in your favor and you are in a position *to maximize any potential sale.* The rules have changed. You are now the home team. You own the equipment, the field, and the crowd. Don't sacrifice the home field advantage.

When a buyer comes to you, the thrust has reversed from "I want to convince you how I can help you" to "Let me provide you with the various options with which I can help you." You have no need to prove credibility, and you have no imperative to cater to the buyer's demands.

A buyer approaching you—no matter what the impetus—is saying, "I've heard good things, I'm willing to believe you can help me, and I'd like your expertise in determining how you can help me." This is a time for boldness. On most occasions, consultants who have been approached leave money on the table because they are so overcome by being sought out that they—against all common sense—become even more malleable and compromising at precisely that point when they can become firmer and more prescriptive. Go figure.

When a true buyer approaches you, for any reason, here are some guidelines to keep in mind in order to maximize the sale and, accordingly, most help the buyer.

Five Techniques to Maximize the Sale when the Buyer Comes Knocking

1. Don't Engage in as Much Diagnosis, and Be Bold in Becoming More Prescriptive. When a key buyer at Merck approached me and I told him that we could jointly examine the situation, he told me, "Alan, I've come to you because I've heard that you can frame this quickly and suggest a resolution. If I wanted to be part of a committee, I could have done that without you." I only needed to hear that once, and it's now burned into my synapses.

2. Always Provide Options. The buyer has already expressed interest, and your options move the buyer from "Should I really do this" to "*How* should I really do this?" That's a subtle but huge psychological leap that enables you to become the de facto choice with just the question of how to use you to be resolved.

3. Find Out What the Budget Is. It's actually quite natural to ask someone approaching you, "Have you allocated an investment for this project?" This will immediately enable you to either inform the prospect that you can't do the project justice for that meager sum, or that you can provide several options (see Step 2) within that budget.

4. Provide One Option Above the Budget. If Steps 2 and 3 work out, then provide two or three options within the budget and one *above* the budget. If the high end denotes sufficient value, the buyer might just find additional money. Buyers hate to increase fees, but they absolutely loathe to lose value. Once you know the budget and can provide options, use one to test the envelope.

> No one likes to be rejected, including buyers. The mere hint that you might not be willing to undertake the project of someone who sought you out will tend to make him or her a lot more flexible and accommodating.

5. Be Prepared to "Walk Away." Nothing has the potential to solidify and guarantee a sale like your expressed willingness to walk away from it. Don't be bashful about saying, "Under the conditions you've outlined, I can't take this on" or "Ethically, I can't undertake this because you seem to have conflicting objectives." When the buyer comes to you, he or she is not prepared to be rejected. (Imagine an auto salesperson saying, "You're not ready for this car, and I can't in good conscience sell it to you.") Your being willing to "walk the higher ground" will influence the client to be more reasonable and to put any discussion of fees on the back burner.

When buyers come to you, as they increasingly should as your "brand" and success grow, don't treat them the same as those buyers whom you are beating the bushes to encounter. Psychologically, the threat of rejection is no longer your concern; it's theirs.

I once told a buyer, quite innocently, that I wasn't sure I could undertake his project, knowing that my calendar was quite full. Before I could offer that explanation, he said, "If it's more money, that's no problem. You can name your fee." I managed to fit him in.

FROM MY TIME IN THE TRENCHES

New business usually must be stalked. The frontal attack is quickest, most economical, and most efficient. When that's impossible, a longer flanking attack may be justified.

When flanking maneuvers don't work or are unavailable, you can still infiltrate an organization in more subtle ways. The combination of these three approach elements should lead you to a buyer at least 75 percent of the time if you're serious, creative, and perseverant. In fact, they will work far better than cold calling, direct mail, and other generic methods.

There are also times when clients come to you, and you must be prepared to exploit the opportunity. There is no sense in leaving money on the table, so take firm and somewhat aloof positions. That is, don't cave in to buyer demands. Instead, cite your own ideal scenarios. There are few ways that ensure a sale as much as a clear signal that you will walk away from one.

Finally, always bear in mind that these machinations are necessary for you to truly help the client. If you ardently believe that you can help people, and you merely have to find ways to enable them to allow you to do that, you'll be successful more often than not.

The first sale is always to yourself.

CHAPTER 3

How to Build Relationships with Economic Buyers

Most Consultants Don't Stop "Selling" Long Enough to Really Make a Sale

When I began my own practice, I wasn't intimidated by the larger consulting firms because I realized that "selling" consulting services was not like selling computers (where people want the best price) or fast food (where people want the quickest service). It was more like selling brain surgery, where people don't care about the price or the wait.

The patient wants the best brain surgeon in the galaxy, because the quality of the service has life-and-death implications.

The more personal the issue, the more emotion-tied the initiative, the more that relationship matters more than money. In twenty-six years of consulting work and travel to fifty-one countries and forty-nine states, I've never seen anyone wash their rental car. There is no emotional attachment. But I've seen people treat their own cars like family members (and sometimes, far better).

Ironically, successful consultants, who have brands, impressive track records, lengthy client lists and references, and all kinds of other assets that accrue to those who have made it, don't bother to emphasize relationship building in the acquisition of new clients. It's as if the skills have atrophied.

At this stage of my career, I find that the partners in McKinsey or Andersen are not the threat to my livelihood, since they're virtually never significant enough principals to impress a buyer. I have much more competition from people like me—owners of boutique firms who are the principals and who do know how to create strong and rapid buyer relationships.

I would suspect that the same holds true for many of you, so the lessons that follow may be the key to the continued flow of lifeblood through your practice.

BEHAVIORAL PREDISPOSITIONS: FUNNY THINGS THAT BUYERS DO

The way to build relationships with buyers is to adjust to their behavioral preferences. We've all made the mistake of trying to make small talk with someone who doesn't want to, or refusing to do so with someone who does. It's one thing to refuse to adjust in a social setting, but it's another to be so stubborn when you want the other person's money.

I've found that all of us have what I call a "comfort zone." This is our most salutary state of being *in a given environment*. Our comfort zones might vary from one setting—business—to another—home, social, civic, and so on. We've all heard the refrain, "You know, you're not at the office now" or "You must be mistaking me for a client," at one time or another.

> Relationship building goes more quickly when you take your time. It's better to find out what the buyer's preferences are rather than assume or, even worse, simply use your own by default. Allow the other person to lead.

The best representation of comfort zones and adjustments that I've found was in the work pioneered by Dr. David Merrill and developed and published by Robert and Dorothy Grover Bolton.[1]

On the line below, place yourself in terms of your normal level of assertiveness in your professional dealings. On the low end, you would tend to be less confrontational, carefully think through decisions, exert less pressure, and allow others to take the initiative. On the higher end, you would tend to exert more pressure, confront readily, be more risk-oriented, and make quick decisions.

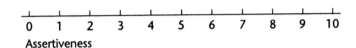

Now, on the vertical line below, place yourself in terms of how emotionally controlled you are, which we'll call "responsiveness." At the top, low end, you would tend to limit gestures, come across as somewhat serious, focus on facts, and be less interested in small talk. On the higher end, you would use dramatic gestures, be highly outgoing and socially initiating, focus on and embrace feelings, and be less concerned about time.

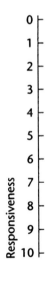

---

1. *Social Style/Management Style: Developing Productive Work Relationships* (New York: AMACOM, 1984).

These two points will intersect in one of four quadrants or grids, shown below. About 25 percent of the general population falls into each quadrant. There are no value judgments made—none are inherently good or bad, strong or weak. Identify the quadrant in which your two points converge.

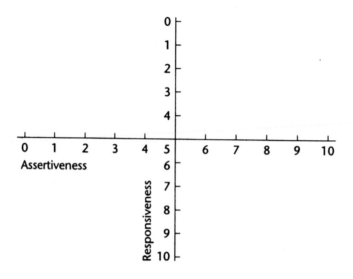

Use behaviors to understand how others might act and respond, not to justify why they're wrong or why you shouldn't listen. If you can invest time in anticipating how buyers will act, you actually shorten the sales cycle considerably.

Here are four quick descriptions of the behavioral types we find in each quadrant (Figure 3.1). I want to emphasize that these shouldn't be "labels" used to explain away behavior ("What do you expect from a woman?" or "How else would someone his age act?"). Rather, these are useful guides to understand your own comfort zone and that of your prospective buyer, so that you can make the adjustments that create common comfort.[2]

2. Discomfort may sometimes be necessary to get people to act, but relationships are built on initial comfort so that trust can be developed, allowing for the admittance of later discomfort.

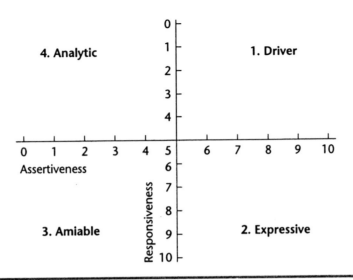

Figure 3.1. Social Styles and Behaviors

Quadrant 1: "Driver" Behaviors

This individual tends to be highly task-oriented. He or she is oriented toward getting things done fast and is much more results-driven than people-driven. This person will probably want to get down to business rapidly and will handle confrontation directly and authoritatively. Reliance in tough situations will be on confidence, presence, and power (formal or personal).

The One That Got Away

An assignment to build a project execution prototype was "sold" to the economic buyer. We were really having a meeting with his VPs to "bless" the project. The fly in the ointment came when we had not educated the organization on criteria to choose the best project manager, and they chose one of the worst. First of all, those types of things should have been cleared before any proposal—and weren't. We had incomplete client conceptual agreement. Second of all, should we have kept our mouths shut and "re-worked" the thinking post-sale? I still have some ambivalence about that—we could have been fired before starting or the project would never have worked. Either way, it was gone.

—Janice Scanlon, President, Accelerate Your Success

Quadrant 2: "Expressive" Behaviors

These people are highly verbal and will easily share emotions. They are natural leaders, formally or informally, and seek the front row and the limelight. They will become aggressive when challenged and despise losing face. They tend to be less comfortable as individual contributors, and much prefer to work with and through others.

Quadrant 3: "Amiable" Behaviors

These individuals are also highly people-oriented, but are more focused on acceptance than on leadership. They tend to avoid confrontation (love relationships but are non-assertive) and will try not to jeopardize relationships at any cost. They therefore would rather provide a qualified or nebulous answer than give an outright "no" and may be hard to move quickly to a decision.

> If the buyer shares your own comfort zone, you don't necessarily have an advantage. Two expressives can be very gregarious, but if they engage in competition for the limelight then that comfort zone becomes very uncomfortable.

Quadrant 4: "Analytic" Behaviors

Analytically oriented people work from a position of respect for their expertise, since that tends to draw people to them and they, themselves, are not outgoing. They will rely heavily on facts and data and tend to eschew all emotionalism in decision making. They prefer facts and documentation to influence and friendships. Analytic buyers will always have clear criteria for their decisions.

To compare these behaviors in a simple reference:

	Driver	Expressive	Amiable	Analytic
Appeal to	Power/ results	Attention	Acceptance	Facts and data
Avoid	Wasting time	Ignoring needs	Threats	Guesswork

	Driver	Expressive	Amiable	Analytic
Response to Confrontation	Authoritative	Aggressive	Acquiescence	Avoidance
Excesses	Domineering	Overbearing	Permissive	Nit-picking
Strengths	Determined	Imaginative	Supportive	Methodical

The key to these "comfort zones" is flexibility. Your ability to identify, adapt, and reflect the other party's preferences is critical during early relationship building. Since so many of us have succeeded through the application of very strong and repeated behaviors, we tend to sublimate our own flexibility and push through our preferences at any cost. That might work in soccer or chess, but it doesn't work well in sales.

Some quick examples:

If you're dealing with a driver, don't force small talk on him or her. But if you're with an expressive, be prepared for lengthy digressions.

Provide an analytic with facts, cross-references, indexes, and comparisons, but give a driver a simple "executive summary" sheet.

Don't drive an amiable toward a decision until all assurances and guarantees are in place. Amiables love references, referrals, and hearing from colleagues in similar situations.

Drivers make decisions, so be prepared for one. They are likely to say, "Okay, let's do it. How much?" Many consultants lose sales *after the driver has forced them to demonstrate how they'll go forward.*

Don't compete with expressives. Give them all the credit, and then some. The check will still be in your name.

Don't become exasperated with analytics. If they need more data, get it. Arguing that they don't need it is like telling your dog he's already had lunch and should no longer be hungry. Dogs can eat non-stop, which is how analytics can consume information.

Listen carefully to expressives and amiables, but be prepared to voice your own views to drivers and analytics. The former two will often say, "What can you do for me?" while the latter two will say, "What can I do for you?" The former want to see what's in it for them; the latter want to assess whether or not to spend any more time.

> The toughest matches are the diagonal opposites. Make a careful effort if you're trying to form one of these relationships. These opposites share virtually no common ground behaviorally.

We'll return to these comfort zones when we discuss basic resistance areas in the next chapter. But for now, consider what your preferred style is, how you'll quickly determine where your buyer is, and how you'll make the connection. It's not rocket science.

It's business acquisition.

Who Could Make This Up?

While working for Hewlett-Packard, I was asked to bid on a major piece of work in competition with the old firm of Ernst & Young. We were the only two being considered.

My competitor and I both showed up at a meeting with six HP managers who controlled the budget. The project was oriented toward helping "re-skill" people so that employees could easily move into jobs in the new organizations that had been formed in the company due to more sophisticated technology. HP has always prized its people, and the "HP Way" is a real and pragmatic philosophy in the company of how to deal with people supportively.

Since Ernst & Young had done the reengineering aspect of the new organizations, I thought that they had a lock on the additional project, until their partner, who was making the first presentation, said, "We handle people the same way we do processes, with templates. If you'll take a look at these, you'll see that we've classified everyone by category and should be able to make rapid decisions about their futures."

I knew immediately that I had the job if I didn't screw up when my turn came. I managed not to.

You have to know your buyer's style, emotional involvement, and beliefs. If you don't, you're just shooting blank bullets into a dark room where there is no target.

—AW

CONTROLLING THE DISCUSSION
(KILLING ME SOFTLY WITH HIS SONG . . .)

Veteran consultants often "play it by ear," meaning that they enter a discussion with a buyer in an exploratory manner, ready to bob and weave or thrust and parry as the conversation develops. That might be effective in boxing or fencing, but since consultative selling is not a contact sport, I'm dubious about the efficacy of those techniques.

All of us have had great successes and great failures in relationship building, but those reading this book have probably had more of the former than the latter. However, I'd maintain that the ratio still isn't high enough, and one of the reasons is that we don't take the time to articulate our own processes. We're good, but we don't know why.

> Make no mistake, it's better to know *why* you're good than *that* you're good. The second allows you to slap your own back. The first allows you to deposit money in the bank.

Here are the red flags that indicate you've lost control of the discussion with a potential buyer. Any one of them spells trouble, but three or more probably mean that the immediate situation is unrecoverable.

Ten Indicators That You've Lost Control of the Discussion
1. You are talking about fees prior to establishing the buyer's objectives.
2. You are doing more than 25 percent of the talking.
3. The buyer is asking questions to satisfy himself about your credibility.
4. The buyer allows for (or has planned) interruptions by an assistant, phone, or other means.
5. You are seated across a desk and the buyer's posture and demeanor would be no different if you were a subordinate.
6. The buyer informs you that he or she has less time than anticipated or that the "new" plan is that you'll spend most of the allotted time with a subordinate.
7. You are constantly defending, instead of explaining, approaches and positions.

8. The buyer tells you that it's "premature" to discuss his or her objectives or needs.
9. Your questions are answered succinctly with no supporting detail, and the buyer never offers any elaboration or independent opinion.
10. There is no resolution or agreement as to next steps.

Consultants lose control of discussions because they don't follow a sequential plan. Since they have no map, they don't know when they're off course. Even in a maze, after all, there is a starting point and an exit point.

Use whatever blueprint suits you, but I have a suggestion for successful people, who should have the confidence, background, and presence to engage in a rather aggressive approach. I call this "accelerating the conversation," and it's intended to move relationships more quickly to either (a) a point where conceptual agreement can be reached and a proposal submitted or (b) a point where you know that it's folly to pursue things any further.

The Blueprint for Controlling a Discussion

1. Set "Min/Max" Objectives for Your Meeting. This means that you determine the maximum and minimum outcomes that you desire from an initial (or subsequent) meeting. (I actually had a consultant in one of my workshops tell me that "I expect a proposal every time, every meeting." I asked if he associated that ridiculous position at all with the fact that his business was struggling.)

A minimum objective might be to reach agreement on some basic needs, frame some general approaches, and formulate more specific questions for a more detailed discussion within a week. A maximum objective might be to set some basic objectives and measures of success, and meet again to discuss variations, options, and the value to the client organization.

If you don't know what to expect from the meeting, then how can you tell whether or not you've been successful?

2. Consider Your "Presence." At this stage of the game, if you're showing up with a huge briefcase, slides, a laptop computer, and other accoutrements of a traveling road show, you're lost somewhere in the Fifties. This isn't how executives visit each other.

Use a brief portfolio or just a pad to take notes. Have you ever seen an executive with a beeper or a phone in a holster on a belt? I never have, and I'd never be seen in public that way. Those are electronic versions of pocket protectors, and the guys with the pocket protectors were keeping the machines running but never in charge of buying new ones. If you have luggage, leave it in the car or at the receptionist's desk.

3. Establish the Objectives with the Buyer.   One of the best opening lines after "hello" (and whatever initial relationship building you might have to do with expressives and amiables) is: "I know your time is valuable and I'm sure you have some objectives for this meeting. I'd like to propose that we begin by sharing what each of us expects to accomplish and then allot our time together accordingly."

It's very powerful to share objective early, so that you:

Immediately establish a peer-level relationship (we're both busy)
Create expectations about time use and priorities
Flush out any incorrect expectations from your prospect
Begin controlling and influencing the discussion subtly but firmly

> You take or lose control of a discussion from the moment you walk in the door. Your appearance, demeanor, and language will quickly tell the buyer whether or not you're a peer or someone to be delegated to a subordinate down the hall.

4. Listen.   You should speak no more than 25 percent of the time. As a general rule, the earlier you are in the relationship, the less you should speak. You learn when you listen. Here are my four favorite listening techniques:

Provocative Questioning. Never ask binary ("yes" or "no" response) questions. Ask reactive questions. Instead of, "Is the downturn in the economy affecting your business yet?" ask "What steps have you taken to insulate yourself from economic uncertainties?" Don't ask, "What is your retention rate?" but rather "What's different today about retaining your top talent compared to five years ago?"

Turnaround Questioning. Never become defensive. It's common for buyers to ask pointed questions such as, "What do you think you can do for us that we haven't already done?" or "Boil it all away—what will your fees be?" The best way to handle these blunt questions is by deflecting them: "I don't know whether I can do anything at all! Will you tell me what you have done, what you'd like to accomplish above that, and then we can compare notes?" Or for fees, "I have no idea what investment would be required, and it would be unfair to you for me to guess. But if you're willing to share your objectives, set some metrics, and establish the impact of the results, I can get you a proposal very quickly, which will provide all of your options and the commensurate ROI."

Reflective Listening. Never "step on" the buyer's narrative. Veteran consultants are especially anxious to share all of their experiences in dealing with the prospect's problems. Instead, simply say, "Is that right?" or "Really?" or "I see" every minute or two. By staying "active" in the discussion to a small degree, you encourage the prospect to continue talking so that you can continue learning. You'll also avoid inadvertent "one-upmanship," which we all hate when it's done to us. ("You think that's a problem? Let me tell you what I faced at the Acme Corporation. . . .")

The Echo Technique. This is merely the habit of repeating the final word a person says. For example, after the sentence, "We've had an interesting time trying to find talent," reply, "Talent?" You'll find that the other person will always respond to a single word of inquiry and expand on his or her thoughts. The echo technique sounds silly, but good listeners use it all the time to prompt others to provide information. (Listen to any really good trial lawyer.)

5. Make Notes. Your ability to quickly frame and summarize the discussion periodically will ensure that you are both on track and will also provide a subtle control of the direction of the interchange. This also shows how much you value the buyer's points and provides a reference for follow-up letters, proposals, and so forth. I've added value to many proposals by going back to my original notes from early meetings and adding the buyer's own words and expectations.

The most effective sales techniques I use are educating the client, listening to the client, and the truth.

I use the client meeting as an opportunity to educate the client in those areas in which the client may not have current and/or accurate information. By providing the information, the response I usually get is favorable. I fill in the gaps in the client's knowledge, even if I don't get the contract at that time. The client knows I am reliable and I keep up-to-date with the latest information. This shows the client that I am more interested in doing a good job rather than just getting the "sale."

Most clients I deal with want to tell a story. I listen without interrupting. This gives the client the feeling that he or she is being heard and begins a more personal development. I then use this prologue to ask questions concerning the project and personnel involved. It's almost like being a detective. I have a picture but now I need more facts. The client usually appreciates the dialogue and I can begin to separate the facts from the perceptions and the "politics."

I have found truth to be the most powerful ally. There is no way around the truth. Either I know something or I don't; either I can do something or I can't. Maybe I'm old-fashioned (I'm 55 years of age), but this is the way I have always worked. I learned this lesson while working for a great former boss early in my career and it has always been a tenet of my consulting practice.

—Leonard Steinberg, CMC

View a discussion as though the two of you were driving together in a car, but you have volunteered to steer. Your passenger can adjust the seat, temperature, radio, and other factors, but you're determining where to go and when to stop. It's tough to jump out of a moving car.

You should be the one pointing out that "We only have about fifteen more minutes, so perhaps we should make plans for our next discussion," rather than the buyer saying, "Oh, sorry, I have to rush off to my next meeting." Your citing the time allows the buyer to either decide to extend it or to agree to your suggestion of another discussion.[3]

Always, Always *End with Some Action Plan You Suggest.* My favored alternative is to provide the buyer with options (a choice of "yeses"). For example, "This was an excellent session, and we both seemed to get quite a lot out of it. I'd like to pursue just a few more points and then we should both be in a position to determine how to go forward. Would you like to set up another date now, or should we do it by phone? I'm available on three separate days next week, and you can choose the best time for you."

If your maximum objectives were met, then tell the buyer that you'll be sending a proposal. If lesser objectives were met, then suggest some options that will take you to the next objective and, ultimately, to a proposal. Never allow a prospect to say, "I'll give you a call." It's better to be assertive to the point of aggressive at this juncture, rather than not have your phone calls returned after a more polite departure.

Once you've determined the comfort zone of your buyer, control the discussion through movement to his or her comfort zone, careful listening, and a pre-established blueprint for setting the course.

EMOTIONAL TARGETING

Logic makes people think, but emotion makes them act. Consultants, with our methodologies, models, matrices, approaches, technology, and graphs, simply tend to over-intellectualize everything.

No one really buys a car because of the features in the brochure. They buy it, no matter what their economic strata, because they look or feel good in it. Only the analytical style, discussed above, might make a choice strictly on objective comparisons, but even there the choice of two or more equally sound alternatives will devolve to a visceral decision.

---

3. Note that although I always favor face-to-face meetings, a strong initial meeting makes it easier to continue with phone calls if you must or if distance is a problem.

The Twilight Zone

Sitting at dinner with the head of purchasing for a very large label manu-facturer and one of my own technical specialists, the conversation took its usual course covering part personal and part business. The specialist and I were forced to do most of the talking, as the head of purchasing was not much of a conversationalist, volunteered little or nothing, and was quite terse in his responses to our questions.

To make things even more uncomfortable, this dinner was to be the moment of truth. After six weeks of product testing, we were about to find out if we were going to get the order. Finally, dessert and coffee arrived and we still had no idea whether or not we had the order.

Not being able to wait any longer, I finally asked how many drums of material he would be needing per month and when he would like delivery to begin. The three of us sat there in silence *for over fifteen minutes.* It was the longest fifteen minutes of my life, as no one spoke a word. All you could hear was some swallowing, chewing, and my sphincter closing up.

At the end of what seemed to be an eternity, the head of purchasing final-ly spoke: "Twenty. In thirty days."

—Jim Altfeld, President, Altfeld, Inc.

If you want to reach an emotional nexus with a buyer, find out "why" something is important, and find out why it's personally important.

How many times have you heard that there are unlimited funds, or peo-ple being shifted around, or all other priorities dropped because a particular ini-tiative is "the boss's baby" or "the general manager has staked his reputation on it" or "she said we would accomplish this or die in the attempt"?

During the relationship-building process, determine why certain objec-tives are important. If you can make those connections, then you'll know what to emphasize in terms of your contributions and results, and the bond should be strengthened.

Ten Questions to Elicit Emotional Priorities

1. Why is this project so important to you, personally?
2. Why is it that you were chosen to lead this (or have chosen to lead this)?
3. How will this reflect on your department?
4. What will be your customers' reaction?
5. Who in the company is evaluating your progress and success with this?
6. What is the extent to which this influences your repute?
7. Does this have a direct career impact for you?
8. If this is successful, what's next in store for you?
9. How does the success of this improve your life?
10. On a scale of 1 to 10, how important is this to you and your position?

The reason that relationship building is so critical is that buyers (or anyone else, for that matter) will not trust you enough to disclose emotional needs until there is a high degree of comfort. Relationship building can *begin* on an intellectual basis, but should progress to emotional disclosure.

One of the best ways to get there rapidly is through self-disclosure. I've often stated to people with whom I'm developing a relationship that I loathe the downsizing trend, and that companies tend to lose too much talent through blind cost reduction formulas. Is that somewhat dangerous or risky? Not if I've read the other party accurately, and it will tend to prompt similar disclosures from the buyer, for example, "And we've had a talent retention problem here that keeps me up at night."

If you're thinking that it's more difficult to gain emotional disclosure from a driver or an analytic, you're right and you've been listening. However, there is absolutely no excuse for not absolutely gaining it from an amiable and an expressive, and at least trying it with the others. Remember, these are comfort zones, not intractable, fenced boundaries. People can cross over, especially if you establish the precedent.

DRAWING A LINE IN THE SAND FOR UNACCEPTABLE BEHAVIORS

Some behaviors are dysfunctional and are rooted in personality disorder. There's no sense trying to build a relationship, since it won't be going anywhere anyway.

These are the behaviors that are an invitation to pack your bags, fold your tent, vacate the premises, and turn out the lights:

Rudeness. When people keep you waiting repeatedly, without apology, when they take non-critical calls and accept interruptions during your meeting and when they insult your opinions or position, just say "Ciao."
Backstabbing. I've had prospects say, "My key objective is to sink that no good son of a bitch Miller over in sales. If we can set him up, you're worth your weight in gold." I'm a consultant, not a hit man.

> There is one thing worse than no business: bad business. You will regret it every waking hour, and it will sap your energy and undermine your morale. No amount of money is worth the pain of dealing with a moron.

Conflicting and/or Unreasonable Objectives. "I want to improve morale while we downsize" is my all-time personal favorite. I told the buyer that the fee would be $5 million. The glazed look on his face is still a fond memory.
Poor Chemistry. Don't laugh, but some people were simply not made to collaborate with each other. For example, passive-aggressive behavior will bring out the worst in most partners. Many supercilious and trivial people will bring the other party down to their level. If it doesn't feel good, don't do it. Easy for me to say? Every veteran reading this book can probably cite several instances of "I wish I had never agreed to do work with him."

In finding the emotional target of the buyer, make sure that your own emotions are positive, supported, and aligned. If they are, you're well on your way to building a great relationship.

FROM MY TIME IN THE TRENCHES

Relationship building is critical to gaining conceptual agreement with prospective buyers about objectives, measures of success, and the value of those objectives to the client organization. Without a relationship, there will be insufficient trust to gain a true disclosure of that information.

Adapting to others' comfort zones is the best way to accelerate relationship building. Flexibility in movement is the key, despite our own comfort zones. Various zones have various influencers, avoidance behaviors, and motivators.

As you gain comfort stylistically, strive to control the discussion. Create a blueprint or road map for the meetings, and subtly but firmly guide the direction, always as a peer of the buyer, and never as a supplicant, "salesperson," or subordinate. Uncover emotional targets, which prompt people to act more quickly and with more commitment, disclosing some of your own emotional factors if it will serve to generate similar revelations from the buyer.

Draw a line beyond which behaviors are unacceptable, no matter what the project or how large the potential. Walk away from troubling business, since it will always undermine you in the long run. Positive and mutually supportive business potential is in abundance, so don't settle for less.

CHAPTER 4

Rebutting Objections Once and for All

If You Hear a New Objection, Then You Haven't Been Listening in the Past

I f a consultant has been actively seeking new business for a year, he or she should have heard about 95 percent of all objections, reservations, demurrals, and skepticism that will be heard for the rest of one's career. The other 5 percent will come as the consultant moves to higher level buyers after reaching success.

For the ultimate consultant, however, that 5 percent has come and gone. I haven't heard a "new" objection in the past ten years.[1] I hear them expressed by different people, in different

---

1. I'm talking about rational buyers. I do occasionally hear that "I don't make these decisions until I contact my deceased uncle" or "I would've done this before the UFO abducted me," but that is, literally, another story.

environments, under different conditions, but once you parse, conjugate, and dissect them, they're the same old reasons.

One of the reasons that veteran consultants leave too much money on the table is that they've become successful despite "blind spots"—types of objections that they've never been able to rebut or turn around and that they've accepted as dead ends. They have convinced themselves, often subconsciously, that certain "magic words" represent defeat and have conditioned themselves to cut their losses. In time of great success and abundance, this deficit can be tolerated, of course. But even forgetting tougher times, when every piece of potential business is vital, what about the fact that one could be making 50 percent or even 100 percent more money by simply eliminating the "blind spots" and snatching victory from the jaws of these formerly inevitable defeats?

What three objections do you, chronically, have the most trouble rebutting (or which three simply cause you to throw up your hands and head for the exit)? Make a note of them on the lines below.

1. _____

2. _____

3. _____

We have all had our own "blind spots," and without some help (which is often hard to find when one is highly successful), they continue throughout our careers, unabated and unreduced. Here are a few examples of the phrases and words that subliminally prepare even the best of consultants for defeat. Are the ones you wrote among them, or in addition to them?

"I have no money, but try us again next year."
"The culture here does not accept external consultants."
"We've tried that in the past and were burned terribly."
"We already have consulting relationships and we're quite pleased."
"We would only use a large, 'name' firm."
"The people you would have to convince are all over the world."
"We're in the middle of two key initiatives, and the timing is awful."
"We have no needs; we're in the middle of unparalleled results."
"Using a consultant is the equivalent of admitting my own incompetence. It's political suicide."

How to Acquire Clients

"We require someone with a staff of at least thirty people."
"We require someone who is within one hour of our home office."

> We don't hear objections we've never heard before. We hear objections we've never been able to rebut before. Those are two very different problems.

THE FOUR MAJOR AREAS OF OBJECTIONS

My experience in sales has been that you can categorize every single objection into one of four areas:

No Trust. In this case, the buyer is simply not comfortable with you. The buyer does not choose to disclose needs, and isn't even comfortable listening to you. The lack of trust may be professional, in that the buyer does not believe there is the competence to resolve the issues, or personal, in that the buyer doesn't like the "chemistry" (or lack thereof) and does not look forward to working with you as a partner.

No Need. The buyer does not feel any reason to use your services. He or she may trust you implicitly, but is not convinced that there are issues to be addressed, or that the issues are the ones you are seeking to address. If buyers don't feel an emotional need, they are unlikely to proceed.

No Hurry. There is no reason to move rapidly. All sense of urgency is missing. The situation is either low priority or is stable. This condition includes "necessary evils" that the company has lived with and tolerated without fatal consequences (not unlike the "blind spots" for consultants noted above!).

No Money. Consultants feel that this is the most common and catholic problem, but it really is the rarest. Everyone has money, and lack of budget is usually an excuse (which buyers realize is the most convincing to otherwise perseverant consultants). This one is often used to prevent conversations and potential relationships from getting under way.

Let's categorize each of the sample objections cited above (NT = no trust; NN = no need; NH = no hurry; NM = no money):

"I have no money, but try us again next year."—NM (But I just want you to go away for now.)

"The culture here does not accept external consultants."—NT (And I don't believe you can overcome that.)

"We've tried that in the past and were burned terribly."—NT (And I don't believe you can overcome that.)

"We already have consulting relationships and we're quite pleased."—NN (And you don't offer anything of additional value.)

"We would only use a large, 'name' firm."—NT (You're not impressive.)

"The people you would have to convince are all over the world."—NH (And it's not worth bringing them together or even asking them about it.)

"We're in the middle of two key initiatives, and the timing is awful."—NH, NN (And the issue you're raising is minor in comparison.)

"We have no needs, we're in the middle of unparalleled results."—NN (And I don't see what benefits you offer.)

"Using a consultant is the equivalent of admitting my own incompetence. It's political suicide."—NT (And I'm not risking my life with you.)

"We require someone with a staff of at least thirty people."—NT (You're too small to do this job.)

"We require someone who is within one hour of our home office."—NT (You're too far away to do this job.)

To arrive at the real objection, you nevertheless have to deal with the superficial objections first. Fortunately, this is fairly easy to do. Unfortunately, many consultants don't bother trying.

Go back to your three toughest objections to rebut. How would you classify them? As a rule, consultants who can't deal with any of these four areas simply fail early; those who can't deal with three will fail slightly later; those who can't deal with two can eke out a living; and those who can't deal with one often become relatively successful, but never achieve their full potential and often leave money on the table. The ultimate consultant has learned how to effectively resolve all four areas of resistance.

BEST PRACTICES

One of the best techniques for closing a presentation or a general sales call is to ask, "Of all the things we discussed in relation to Product/Service X and your company/situation, Ms. Client, what makes the most sense/resonates the most?" Be prepared for some silence as the client reflects on the meeting. What happens next is very interesting.

The client usually says, "I like X and Y." That tells you whether your main points were communicated or not. If there are two clients present, after the first one speaks, slowly prompt the other to share his views. Usually, he will agree or emphasize other features or benefits that appealed to him. They may even disagree on which points are best—which is fine, since they are essentially selling themselves on your proposals. If they are positive, it is then very easy to say, "Great. Sounds like you see the value here. These would be the next steps."

If there are any negatives, then you are there to address them and, again, move to the next appropriate step. In any case, what the client says are benefits and value are more important than what you say are benefits and value and this is a very easy, low-risk, low-pressure way to move forward in the business relationship.

—Anne Miller, author, *365 Sales Tips for Winning Business*,
President, Chiron Associates

REBUTTING ARGUMENTS IN THE FOUR BASIC AREAS

When you hear an objection or even sense resistance, the first thing to do is to categorize it into one of the four basic areas (Figure 4.1). The reason is this: If a buyer feels no need, then no amount of trust building on your part can change that. If a buyer feels no trust, then creating a higher sense of urgency won't help (or will simply send the buyer more rapidly into the arms of another consultant whom he does trust). This is why the stereotypical image of salespeople hopelessly reciting features and benefits is such an accurate picture of real sales futility.

> Any social style may have any major objection. But they do tend to be correlated around comfort zones (or lack thereof). Consequently, identifying a buyer's style should also forewarn you about likely objections.

Note that the four areas correspond somewhat to our social styles of buyers. The correlation isn't 100 percent, but we're often going to find the following:

Drivers must be convinced of need quickly: "How will this help me meet my goals?" Expressives must trust you, because the relationship is so important. Amiables prefer guarantees and assurances to speed, and the cardinal sin is impetuosity and rashness. Analytics want to see returns on investment and are readily convinced that existing plans have been carefully arrived at and should not be changed.

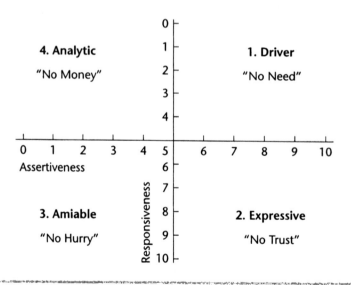

Figure 4.1 Objections as Correlated with Social Style

Here are some diagnostics to help with each area. You might want to focus on the one or two that have presented the most difficulty for you, but you might also find that your more "comfortable" areas can also accept some increased ammunition.

No Need

Indicators

> Buyer does not disclose information
> You're constantly asked "But why should we do this?"
> Buyer wants to know the ROI
> Buyer cites his or her own pressing time demands
> Buyer asks, "Why this approach?" and "How will you help us?"

> Insanity is usually defined as "doing the exact same thing over and over while expecting different results." If buyers aren't responding to your rebuttals, then the rebuttals are the problem, not the buyer.

Consultant Actions

> Make a case for how the buyer and organization will improve, *not for why you're good*. The latter deflects the conversation to you, and you can never be good enough, especially for a driver. Rather, show how the buyer's needs (and particularly use of time and use of power) will be enhanced. Be very concise.
> Focus on the buyer's stated goals, not your methodology. If the buyer is reluctant to disclose, use provocative questioning.
> Cite examples of client organizations and results (the more familiar to the buyer, the better) to give a sense of what other respected parties have deemed important, and find out how the buyer responds.
> State: "To make the best use of your time, there are just four things I'd like to know. Then you can ask me anything you like and I'll be in the best position to answer you substantively." Then ask your four most important questions in that setting ("What is the fundamental issue you wish you could solve tomorrow?").

The buyer says, "I haven't looked at it that way before. Go on."

The buyer begins to disclose details of his or her issues

The buyer offers to extend your time together or set up another meeting

The buyer asks you for ideas on how you would proceed

The buyer exhibits a sense of humor (this is a great sign from a driver)

The One That Got Away

From losing some business, I've learned the power of personal relationship and data. The mix is very important for closing a sale.

When I can be face to face with a client and reflect that I really hear and understand the issues and needs, then provide data about myself, the power of the solution I am suggesting, and good references that are meaningful to the client, I can feel very certain of closing a sale.

When I haven't closed it, usually one of these aspects has been missing.

—Andrea C. Zintz, Ph.D., Andrea Zintz and Associates, LLC

No Trust

Indicators

The buyer keeps asking about your credentials and background

Questions are deflected and you're continually asked about yourself (as opposed to your professional analysis of the buyer's situation)

The buyer "name drops" and tacitly indicates that he or she has partnered with very prestigious people in the past

You are told about superficial issues (retention down in a tough labor market), but not underlying issues (the reduction in benefits due to cost cutting has directly affected retention)

There are other people invited to the meeting who readily, and even assertively, question you and your ability to be of help

Consultant Actions

Never attempt to rush to business; answer questions completely and, whenever possible, with examples and anecdotes

Ask a lot of questions of the buyer about background, how she wound up in that position, where he's from, and so on

If there are others present, include them in the conversation, while maintaining your primary focus on the buyer

Find points of commonality, no matter how seemingly trivial—vacation spots, schools, work history, acquaintances, hobbies—whatever it takes to demonstrate that you are more similar to the buyer than dissimilar[2]

Listen, listen, listen. Let the buyer talk. Ask questions that encourage the buyer to talk. Expressives actually become more comfortable with strangers when they are encouraged to talk about themselves.

Buyers can get quite comfortable with someone who merely listens well. I've been called a "great conversationalist" when all I've done is asked a few well-timed questions and otherwise kept my mouth shut.

Indicators That You've Succeeded

You're asked to go for coffee, have lunch, or engage in some similar "social" activity

The buyer initiates the move from background and comfort to business and projects

The buyer admits to gaffes and mistakes he or she has made in the past

The buyer confides an organizational weakness, often predicated with, "This is confidential, but . . ."

The buyer extends your time together or sets up another meeting on the spot

---

2. I believe that this transcends gender, race, and ethnicity. We all have far more in common than uncommon in our humanity. The mistake we often make, however, is to focus on differences.

The Twilight Zone

Probably many consultants have experienced this. Our work is business planning and strategy development for aircraft industry manufacturers and suppliers.

A major supplier that provides material to all the aircraft manufacturers called us to talk about future demand for commercial aircraft. I discussed how we could assist them, but at the end of the day, our conclusions would not be very different than the information they receive for free from Boeing, Airbus (and, then, McDonnell Douglas). I suggested they just use what they were getting and not incur the expense of a specialized evaluation.

Two days later, they called back to say that our honesty and directness convinced them that we could help them sort through their issues with the material they were receiving. This relationship led to repeat engagements over five years.

All because I told the client they didn't need a consultant!

—Gerald W. Bernstein, Managing Director,
Stanford Transportation Group

No Hurry

Indicators

The buyer asks for assurances, guarantees, and references

The buyer seeks to involve more people, form a task force, assemble a committee

Minute details are discussed at length, and meetings run longer and longer

Decisions that you thought had already been made are revisited, and vacillation occurs frequently

The buyer talks in terms of "pilots," tests, and "beta" groups

Consultant Actions

Provide references and testimonials from people who have implemented the same project or similar methodology

Provide "fail safe" options so that there are alternatives in place to handle setbacks

Establish both preventive and contingent actions to safeguard the plan (for example, project planning is preventive, delaying one of the steps is contingent if something goes wrong anyway)

Demonstrate that the current situation is actually declining, not stable, and it will be harder and harder to recover the longer the buyer waits to implement

Offer to provide a briefing as a prophylactic move with the buyer's boss

Guarantee the quality of your work (not the results, which is impossible and unethical)

> The "timing" will never be perfect. What you have to prove to a buyer is that the timing can get a hell of a lot worse very quickly.

Indicators That You've Succeeded

The buyer moves forward against a joint and methodical plan; prior decisions are not revisited

The buyer agrees that risk is minimized

Your meetings are increasingly one-on-one, without others present to comment or gain consensus

The buyer agrees that a test would just waste time or consume resources unnecessarily

The buyer readily agrees to be the chief sponsor and to lend his or her name to the project (as opposed to naming a project manager)

No Money

Indicators

The buyer says that this initiative isn't budgeted, and he or she doesn't know where the funds will come from

Strict ROI calculations are demanded

There is an attempt to peg your fee to the actual return or savings

The buyer stipulates that anecdotal measures aren't sufficient

The buyer tells you, "We've never spent money on this type of project" (or on outside consultants)

Consultant Actions

Provide details of cost savings from similar projects at other organizations

Focus on value, not fee; sell the buyer on the ultimate worth, and deflect all discussions about fee

Stress investment, not cost

Point out the preventive investment in equipment and machinery that the organization makes every day

Offer a money-back guarantee on the quality of your work

Offer options (various value "packages") so that the buyer can please himself as to ROI

Provide cross-indexed, tabulated documentation with footnotes and references

Indicators That You've Succeeded

The buyer indicates a favorable/acceptable return ratio

The buyer asks that you "sharpen your pencil" and come back with your best possible offer

The buyer wants to get into further levels of detail

The buyer creates charts, diagrams, flow charts, mind maps, and similar aids to the discussion

The buyer suggests details for implementation and wants to pursue the references

---

The good news is that there are really only four basic areas of objection. The bad news is that, if you don't know how to handle one or two, you're going to be doomed to mediocrity, no matter how successful you've been to date.

The four basic resistance areas are immutable. They've existed since an ancient stone salesman approached a Pharaoh for the next pyramid construction contract. They correlate closely, although not perfectly, with the social styles of buyers. Remember that there is NO objection that we haven't heard before. If we prepare, are sensitive to the indicators, and respond to that particular style and objection, we are highly likely to move the relationship and sale forward at sprint speed.

VISUALIZING THE FUTURE

I'm going to offer here a technique that I've never written about in any of my books and seldom speak about in my workshops. It may seem "new age" or, as Ron Zemke, a terrific writer, has termed, the "woo-woo" effect. But it works, and it serves to rebut objections with the force of a Pete Sampras return of a second serve.

In any meeting I've ever entered, I try to visualize what might transpire. As we all progress in this profession, our experience base enlarges and our ability to anticipate becomes rather comprehensive. I can't remember the last time something occurred in a sales call or client meeting of any type that surprised me.[3]

When you approach a meeting with a prospect, visualize what he or she might say (if you know the person's style already, you can narrow this down considerably). Then develop responses to the objections that seem extemporaneous, but which are really "rehearsed."

Here are the specific techniques that you can employ when you visualize the future:

Prepare Alternatives. State, "That's a good point, and there are three things to consider. . . ." This demonstrates tremendous command of the issue and will focus the buyer on which of the considerations are most important.
Prepare Comparisons. State, "That's exactly what happened during my work at Boeing, and here's what we did about it." This demonstrates that you're experienced in the prospect's concern and that you can readily deal with it.

---

3. Although I was thrown off balance when a female vice president, reacting to my suggestion that current practices could land the management team in jail, shouted, "I can't go to jail! I might meet my ex-husband in jail!"

Prepare Counterarguments. State, "That is a drawback, but it's minor when you consider these four significant advantages." This demonstrates that you've done the risk analysis, and that it's manageable.

Prepare Collaboration. State, "Yes, that is a significant challenge, and I think that you and I personally have to spend some time resolving it." This highlights the partnership and demonstrates that your combined talents are needed for success.

Prepare Analysis. State, "That is always an important consideration, and I've prepared some documents for you to review that should alleviate that concern." This demonstrates your foresight and preparedness.

The greater your experience base, the easier it is to use the past to predict the future. Ultimate consultants should reach a point where every conversation is mostly predictable, and most responses become natural and seem extemporaneous, despite the fact they've been "rehearsed" a few minutes prior.

By visualizing the future, you'll be able to anticipate and co-opt prospect objections. It's almost unforgivable to be "blindsided" by an objection for which you are unprepared and have not visualized. At one client, I so often said, "Well, there are five things we can do here," that the president actually announced to his staff, "I just love it when he does that! Why can't all of you do that?!"

SAMPLE OBJECTIONS AND REBUTTALS

I've included here a compendium of objections I've heard and rebuttals I've used over the years. They are meant to serve several purposes. First, you might just read some reactions that you wish you had thought of before. Second, you might find that your current responses are as good as or better than mine, which at least tells you you're on the right track. Finally, you might want to use these as practice with your staff, subcontractors, alliance partners, and so on.

Who Could Make This Up?

A colleague and I had collaborated on a project for Texaco. We were working all over the country, but periodically had to visit headquarters in White Plains, New York, where our buyer was an expressive who was "off the chart."

The three of us were taking a walk on the jogging path that ran around the sumptuous grounds, because the buyer loved to be seen shepherding the consultants around. Suddenly, around a turn, appeared an executive vice president of great repute and power.

The buyer excused himself and went off to chat with the vice president for several minutes while my colleague and I cooled our heels watching the ducks paddle around a pond. When the buyer returned, he said, "The vice president told me that the project was going beautifully, and no one could have pulled this off the way that I have."

After we parted company, my colleague observed as we headed for our cars, "A typical expressive—when he can't get applause outright, he applauds himself!"

—AW

Objection I've never heard of you before.

Rebuttal I hear that all the time. I'm a "well kept secret." In fact, my firm is a boutique firm that takes on select clients. It doesn't surprise me that we're not a "household name" because that isn't our strategy.

Objection We think we need a large firm. You're a one-person show.

Rebuttal What you need is careful and meticulous attention, and I'm ideally prepared to provide it. You'll always be dealing with the principal, we don't have a huge infrastructure that demands inflated fees, I'm virtually immediately responsive, and I can tightly customize approaches just for you. How many larger firms can offer you those advantages?

Objection I think there's a lot of potential, but the timing isn't right.

Rebuttal One thing I can guarantee: The timing will never be right. The real question is will the timing improve or decline? Let me make a case that you would have been better off acting six months ago, and six months from now you'll wish you had acted six months prior.

Never, ever get defensive. Instead, become adept at saying, "That's a good point, and one I've faced before. Let me explain what's happened at other clients." If you can't use your past experience to promote future success, what good is it?

Objection We're having a great year. We're on a roll. There's nothing to "fix."

Rebuttal That's why we should talk. My best clients "raise the bar" during periods of strength. None of us improves by correcting weakness. We improve by building on strengths. You're in that wonderful position where you can afford the investment and the prudent risk to attempt new heights. I'm in a position to help you do that. Don't you think we should at least explore that kind of exponential growth opportunity?

Objection There is resistance to external consultants here. In fact, it's strongly countercultural. I don't know if I want to risk swimming against that tide.

Rebuttal I don't blame you. But we're not close to that determination. Let's talk about your key issues and what might be done about them. Then you'll be able to judge whether it's worth the energy to take that swim. For now, we're only exploring hypothetically.

Objection We have no money. It's that simple.

Rebuttal Isn't that a Xerox machine over there? How many of those does the organization own? Maybe a hundred? What is the maintenance contract on those? Maybe $75,000? Are you really saying that preventive maintenance on machinery is justified, but investment in people and performance isn't? How much are you spending on "failure work," which we could eliminate with an intelligent approach? If you're willing to talk in terms of ROI, I can help you make money.

FROM MY TIME IN THE TRENCHES

Accept objections as a sign of interest. Prospects who are totally uninterested wouldn't waste their breath. They are a normal—even necessary—aspect of the sales process. It's your decision whether to see them as hurdles to be negotiated or as mountains that thwart your progress.

There are four major areas of resistance: no trust, no need, no hurry, no money. We too readily accept the fourth, whereas it's actually the least valid and seldom the actual impediment. If you establish trust and need, "no hurry" and "no money" tend to fade away. Learn the predispositions of your buyers and you'll know what kinds of objections to anticipate and rebuttals to prepare.

Visualize your conversations, using your experience to create the likely alternative paths the discussion might take. Introduce what seem like "extemporaneous" observations, which are, in reality, rehearsed responses to the predicted path. After a while, these will become quite natural and "codified," because there is very little new under the sun. If you continue to hear objections that you haven't heard before, you just haven't been listening.

Provide reinforcement for buyers according to the predispositions: power for drivers, recognition for expressives, guarantees for amiables, and detail for analytics. If you follow the natural course of your buyer's preferences, combined with the likely direction of the conversation, you'll accelerate the relationship and the acquisition of new business.

CHAPTER 5

Sixteen Great Acquisition Sources

Why Go Around the Block to Get Next Door?

We all tend to stick with the person who brought us to the dance. That's why so many people become specialists with no real intent to do so. We solicit clients along the paths of least resistance. If we land a couple of car dealers and can use their referrals and our experiences to acquire more, we suddenly become auto distribution experts and consciously or unconsciously focus our marketing efforts in that area. Before we know it, we're locked out of other areas because we're seen as "someone else's specialist" or we've lost the knack for breaking down new doors.

Early in my career I accidentally acquired several pharmaceutical firms as clients and was heading down that slope when, with equal serendipity, I obtained several newspapers as clients. When I sat down one day and analyzed just how different those two industries are in almost every dimension, yet how similar my advice was because my processes are cross-industrial, I realized that I shouldn't stop there. Yet the advice I was getting at the time from "experts" was that I should choose which area to specialize in and abandon the other!

The same principle applies to the sources of our new business. If we've tended to rely on publishing to draw prospects, and it's been successful for us, then the best we do is to seek out new publishing vehicles. If networking has been the key, then we network with a wider focus. If alliances have brought in business, we look for more and larger partnerships.

However, there's nothing wrong with examining new sources of business acquisition. In fact, there are two terrific reasons to do so:

1. You can continue your current "comfortable" paths, since the two approaches are not mutually exclusive.
2. At a successful time in your career, you're better equipped than ever to be credible instantly in new acquisition areas. In other words, these are new routes you tend to "mature into."

Some of the suggestions below will be the current path for some readers. But I doubt there is a single reader who is habitually traveling all sixteen, nor is there a need to do so. The opportunity being offered here is to choose two or three that you haven't tried and to open up an entirely new source of business acquisition *in addition to* your current methods.

Being successful doesn't mean that you stop experimenting with new approaches. It means that you now have the ability and resources to take more of a leap and to experiment with greater gusto. Like Microsoft or Boeing, you can withstand some setbacks.

Here are the highest potential acquisition avenues I see for successful consultants:

1. Partnering with professional colleagues
2. Harvesting low-hanging fruit

How to Acquire Clients

3. Using the Internet in reverse
4. Becoming the "middle man"
5. Publishing "unpromotional" articles
6. Serving the cause for free
7. Taking global vacations
8. Writing on the op-ed page
9. Franchising the talent
10. Pursuing your clients' vendors
11. Developing a memorable brand phrase
12. Selling to your suppliers
13. Infiltrating trade associations
14. Obtaining a profound endorsement
15. Writing The Book
16. Getting a referral every time

THE FIRST FOUR

1. Partnering with Professional Colleagues

I found my attorney through my real estate broker. I found my accountant through my attorney. I found subcontractors through my accountant.

Do key professional colleagues really know what you do, and are they able to endorse you? My relationship banker introduced me to executives within her institution who ultimately hired me for almost $200,000 worth of work. Since she approved my credit line and had to know my business intimately, she was in a perfect position to recommend me with confidence to others, inside or outside the bank.

This occurs too often by accident more than by design. On the local level, at this point in our careers, we all deal with attorneys (and maybe several for trademark, estate planning, litigation, and so on), doctors, accountants, realtors, architects, designers, and bankers. On a wider level, we deal with publishers, editors, brokers, coaches, and association leadership. Have you ever referred someone to your doctor or accountant? Have you expected something in return? Of course you have, and you haven't. You thought you were doing both parties a favor by connecting need with talent.

People should be doing the same for you. The trouble is that you know what your doctor does, but he or she might not have more than a foggy idea of what you do (people to this day look at me quizzically and mumble, "Consultant??").

Action Step: Choose a dozen professional colleagues who provide you with a service and make sure that you informally but clearly educate them about what you do, how you do it, and how to reach you (for example, leave your web address or a copy of your book). Just two referrals a year from these sources can add hundreds of thousands of dollars to your business.

2. Harvesting Low-Hanging Fruit

We're all familiar with the organizations that inform us that "We don't hire consultants." (In the prior chapter, we dealt with rebuttals to that song.) However, we don't pay attention to the converse: There are organizations that love consultants and can't get through a day without them.

Why aren't you getting paid by some of them?

There is a belief that an organization doing business and maintaining a relationship with a consultant is hard to crack by a rival, because the current resource has solid support and history. That's often true. But I'm talking about organizations that use *multiple* consultants at once. These prospects aren't hooked into a single resource; they are hooked into the very idea of utilizing outside help.

> You have enough resistance to overcome. Why not go where you know there is one less barrier, one lower hurdle, one more door ajar?

Sometimes, the very best companies are heavy users of consultants because they know that they need constant fresh air.[1] I had found at one point,

---

1. "We get tired of breathing our own exhaust," says Marilyn Martiny, one of my very best buyers at one of my very best clients, Hewlett-Packard.

for example, that Merck, Hewlett-Packard, and Times-Mirror Group were significant users of consultants, while Bank of America, Hasbro, and large law firms were not. I pursued, through my normal marketing devices, those organizations who required one less sale: They didn't need to be converted to the use of my kind of help.

So, even though Hasbro is in my backyard, and HP is across the country, I went after the easier sale. Those who already believe in the efficacy and cost-effectiveness of outside consultants represent lower hanging fruit, requiring less marketing effort.

Action Step: Take an hour or so with your feet up on the desk and simply think about the organizations that tend to use your competitors in large degree and who fit well into your marketing comfort zone. Make a plan to pursue them. This is like a battleship training the main turrets in a slightly different direction. The ammunition remains the same.

3. Using the Internet in Reverse

People use the Internet to sell and to advertise. You've probably received today, alone, a dozen or more pieces of spam urging you to invest your money, buy irresistible addresses, or lose weight before the end of the day. You've also probably visited your share of websites this week that are nothing more than electronic billboards telling you how great their authors are and sharing with you the kinds of features and benefits that drive you to shut down your browser and sell your computer.

I use the Internet with a "reversed flow." I provide value. For free. My website has almost one hundred free, indexed articles for people to access and download. I provide a free electronic newsletter on life balance (which has grown in three years from forty original names to more than four thousand all over the world). I send out leads and techniques to people on several different lists I maintain.

I bought my first set of the *Encyclopaedia Britannica* when I was very young and had no money. Yet the salesman offered a "free Renoir reproduction" for just listening. He offered value to get to the next step, a discussion. I regretted the expense but gained from the insight.

> You get people's attention by offering something, not asking for something. Don't show them your vacation slides. Offer to look at theirs. You can't sell anything if you can't get in the door.

Use the wonderful reach of the Internet to offer value, in whatever form makes sense for you. Don't maintain an ad site or promote yourself relentlessly in everything you send out. If you offer people value—ideas, tips, techniques, freebies, articles, newsletters, and so forth—they will mention your name, inquire about your work, and buy your services.

Action Step: Review your website and electronic offerings today (or have someone else do it objectively) and determine how much value versus how much self-promotion you're supporting. Then change the percentage to 80/20. You'll find that you have to "give" to "get," but that it's painless.

4. Becoming the "Middle Man"

Sometimes acting as the connection between two parties can be quite lucrative. But I'm not talking about the traditional "broker," who is really unnecessary, yet wants a piece of the action for putting you together with a prospect. These are merely dating services and add very little value.

No, I'm talking about being the *process* or the link that connects people. For example, I maintain a subcontractor list, called the Summit Resource Catalog. There is a modest fee ($50) to join, but it's one-time and people can stay on the list forever. The list is sent for free to firms interested in hiring subcontractors, and they can browse the list by specialty, geography, fee level, and so on.

I get nothing from this transaction and serve only as the connection. Due diligence is up to both parties. The entry fee pays for the administration and mailings. However, as the central source, people at both ends are attracted to me. They have to visit my website, where they are introduced to more value, as well as to products and opportunities to learn about my work. The list has a "word-of-mouth" attraction, so I receive inquiries about it daily.

By serving as a disinterested third party, you become the road that travelers must take to get from one point to another. People are drawn to you as a vital connection, and your own services and talent become peripheral benefits. As a success in your field, you have gained the credibility and means to serve in such a capacity.

Action Step: Make a list of the kinds of people you can uniquely put together, be they readers and publishers, managers and coaches, or veterans and neophytes. Establish a cost-effective mechanism for doing that. Don't take an active role— you should simply be doing other people a good deed. Your turn will come.

The One That Got Away

While working on a proposal for a healthcare institution that I had done some work for in the past, I discovered I had taken for granted the relationship that I had built. The proposal was for a new information system for one of the departments. I had done some work for some of the executives of the hospital for a number of years. The work was always in excellent standing with the board members.

Because of this I was, you can say, "overly confident" that I was going to get the next bid that I put in. I thought my relationship was good enough to carry me to the end and I wouldn't need to put on a big sales presentation on how good I was for this project.

Needless to say, I was wrong. My competition came in and took the bid from right under me. They put on an outstanding presentation and had very good subject-matter experts to back them up. I did a fair presentation without much effort. BIG MISTAKE.

I came in second for the bid. I lost that one and learned a very big lesson. Yes, you can do good work and yes, you can prove yourself, and yes, forming relationships with your client is crucial to success. But DO NOT take the relationship for granted. Always go out of your way to show your stuff and prove that you're the right person for the job. By showing enthusiasm for each bid, you continue to show your professionalism and expertise in the consulting field. You'll be taken seriously and continue on the road to success.

—John Micallef, CBT Consulting Inc.

THE SECOND FOUR

5. Publishing "Unpromotional" Articles

Consulting to Management is a quarterly journal distributed to consultants all over the world. A year or so ago, it ran an article I wrote on mentoring, which featured the details and working of my own mentoring program. Since the program is oriented toward consultants, this was a piece of publicity that I gladly would have paid for. (A sidebar to the story described how to enter my program, including all contact information and requirements.)

> If you offer enough value to the reader and the editor, it's amazing just how much subtle promotion will slip through the editorial cracks. I've had articles and interviews published that embarrassed even my wife in their praise.

Not enough people publish, and of those who do, too many are blatantly self-promotional. The key to business acquisition is to provide a valuable, factual, and objective piece that, oh, by the way, uses your personal history, examples, and accomplishments. Even better are interviews in which you are not even the author, but the subject of a third party's legitimate interest. (I *am not* talking about those dreadful "infomercials" or the fake interviews that are actually scripted and are as transparent as an open window.)

Have you ever purchased a book because of its review and your respect for the reviewing source? Have you ever done something on the recommendation of a trusted friend or advisor? At this stage of your career, you're in the perfect position to offer sage advice and dispassionate help. In so doing, people will flock to you for more of it.

Action Step: Make it a goal to publish and to be interviewed once every quarter as an expert who is cited for accomplishments and experiences (or can cite his or her own) that will attract new business. Gurus are simply people who have had the opportunity to learn from their successes and failures.

6. Serving the Cause for Free

I serve on local boards for the contribution I can make and for my belief in the organization and/or the people who have asked me to help. However, there is no conflict I know of between doing good work and accepting business that might flow from it.

While serving on the board of a shelter for battered women, I happily took the lead in areas of my competency, including board governance, strategy, ethical issues, and so on. One day a fellow board member, who was also a local police chief, asked me if I could impart some of the same competencies to his senior officers as part of their national accreditation requirements. "Don't even ask," he said, smiling, "we have a grant that will pay for it."

I've found from my legitimate and well-intentioned volunteer work on boards that I've gained clients, accelerated word of mouth, and received unexpected media publicity. I've chosen to do this at the local level, even though my historic thrust has not been among local businesses. You may decide to do things on a more national level (an excellent entry point is board membership in professional and trade associations at the national level). When I served as president of a local board for professional speakers, I found that I gained almost $250,000 over the next two years directly attributable to that visibility.

Action Step: As you network, make it known that you're entertaining offers to serve on boards. Choose those that offer a cause you believe in, are well-established, and have a need for your contribution. Do good, and good will follow (supposedly uttered by George Merck, one of the founders of the great pharmaceutical giant).

7. Taking Global Vacations

I don't believe that you compartmentalize your life. Our personal and professional lives add up to one life, with continuing overlap. Why fight that? Embrace it.

You can afford the best of vacations at this point in your career. When you schedule that trip to Hong Kong or Berlin or Buenos Aires, write ahead to the local management groups, associations, branches of your U.S. clients, and personal contacts. Let them know that you'll "be in the neighborhood" and offer to extend your stay if you can be of any assistance.

Who Could Make This Up?

I was talking to the CEO of a client with whom I had done business for five years. We were good friends.

He mentioned casually to me, "Do you know anyone who is a good keynote speaker?" Being one myself, but somewhat skeptical, I asked why he wanted to know.

"Oh," he said, "I've been the program chair of the American Council of Life Insurance for some time, and I'm looking for someone to address 250 CEOs at our annual meeting."

After I convinced him that I was the perfect candidate, I went out and hit myself over the head for never, ever having told him about my speaking and never having asked him about referrals within the industry. I immediately began to comb through the rest of my clients to determine where else I had been so deficient.

How many of your clients are seeking expertise elsewhere because they are unaware that you possess it?

—AW

When you're traveling a long way, you have credentials, and you have some local contacts, you have to deliberately not want to do business locally in order to avoid it. The farther you go, the easier it gets. Of course, you "gotta wanna."

There is an inverse proportion to distance and desire: The farther you are traveling, the more you will be accommodated. If you're going to be in Tokyo for a few days of vacation, then why not add two days of meetings, presentations, or speeches? It's never burdensome, the local hosts will show you and your partner sights you wouldn't have otherwise seen, and you'll develop significant business potential.

I was asked to keynote a consulting conference in Australia. I asked only for a single first-class ticket (these groups are always strapped for cash). They agreed readily. I took my wife on a free ticket and set up the meetings, speeches, and contacts well in advance around my speech. The result was six figures in business and a wonderful trip.

Action Step: Take one vacation a year internationally that can tie in with some local contacts, speeches, book signings, meetings, and so forth. Plan four to six months in advance for maximum impact. At the very worst, you'll have a great vacation.

8. Writing on the Op-Ed Page

When you've got the "traction" of success going for you, you're able to appear in places that were closed to you as a beginner or unknown. One such place is the "op-ed" page of newspapers.

Opposite the editorial page is where opinions are expressed by those whom the newspaper wants to expose to its readers for purposes of interest, provocation, diversity, and other reasons. By offering commentary for this page, you establish yourself as an authority, broadcast your credentials, gain a reprint for your press kit, and allow other media sources to contact you.

When you write on a sensitive business issue—downsizing, retention, ethics—you will gain the attention of the educated, informed, and potential buyers who tend to read those columns. You'll be invited to speak to their teams, to write for their publications, to discuss the issues with them. A newspaper's mere publishing of your piece—even though not necessarily endorsing it—is a tremendous statement of credibility and authority.

You can also judge by the response or lack of response to your piece what the current level of interest is on your topic. I use this to "calibrate" my approaches. If my best provocation can't generate substantial response, then I'm tackling an issue that's important only to me and that's not a business acquisition issue.

Action Step: Submit an article for consideration on the op-ed page at least every other month. Don't feel limited to your hometown newspaper. When these are successful, it's not unusual to be asked to write a column.

The Twilight Zone

In the early Eighties, I was a senior management consultant in the consulting division of a Big 5 (then 10) accounting firm. We received a strong lead from an audit partner in another city, who had a large food and grocery retailing client in need of an operations analysis.

I made the call with the local partner, and all seemed to be going well, until we met the owners. They were three partners who, after surviving the concentration camps in WW II, vowed they would never be reliant on anyone ever again. They felt I had all the qualifications they were looking for except one: I was not of the Jewish faith. They insisted that the engagement be managed by a Jew, or they would not proceed.

The audit partner met with me outside and asked if I had any problem with their request. I said no problem at all, since I could only imagine the horrors they had to endure. I said, "Find a Jewish partner, and let's get on with it!"

That's where the problem began. Believe it or not, we could not find a Jewish consulting partner on the entire East Coast, or an audit partner with time available (it was tax season) to fill in as a substitute. Eventually, they found a twenty-two-year-old staff "B" auditor, recently out of college, as the only available "manager."

We took him back with us to the client, hoping they would not consider this an insult to their request. They interviewed this bright, understanding young man and gave us the immediate go-ahead. I reported to him for the next two months, and although he had no idea what it was I was doing (he was a tax student), he made all my recommendations personally to the client.

The engagement was an outstanding success!

—Tom Casey, CMC, Business Consulting Service

THE THIRD FOUR

9. Franchising the Talent

Some of the work we've all done quite successfully has been routinized to the point where we do it in "unconscious competency." The bad news is that we're no longer as conscientious or innovative at delivering, but the good news is that the work is probably eligible to be "franchised" to others.

Here are some "deliverables" that are candidates to be franchised to other consultants, creating an entirely new business source for you:

Tests and diagnostic instruments you've created
Systematized approaches to team building, strategy, and so on
Workshops oriented around proprietary materials
Manuals, templates, checklists, and review systems
Train-the-trainer programs
Remote coaching and counseling systems
Valuation, assessment, and risk management procedures

> Some business acquisition sources can be established through the creation of new distribution channels, using material and approaches that no longer rely on your personal talent or delivery.

Franchising is especially desirable in areas where there can be little competition, for example, in other parts of the world, granting either local rights for a country or exclusive rights for an entire region. It's also highly efficient in those parts of your practice that are causing you too much labor investment, too much boredom, and/or too little profit. In effect, you create a new business source by creating a "middle man" who will probably deliver better than you have been delivering.

Action Step: List those aspects of your practice that you find are lock-step repeatable and that don't require your talent to sell or deliver. Then decide whether you want to franchise completely, or only on a "non-compete" basis. At this stage in your career, your "brand" can make franchising highly valuable.

10. Pursuing Your Clients' Vendors

The auto industry is famous for demanding that its suppliers adhere to the same strict quality criteria that they do (which doesn't always make sense, but still carries tremendous pressure). For example, Ford may require its brake lining vendor to implement a quality package similar to one used within the Ford system.

Suggest to your existing clients, including brand new ones, that you're more than willing to contact all key suppliers to introduce them to the type of project you're implementing within your client's system. Be prepared to demonstrate the tremendous synergy of sharing, for example, identical planning systems, leadership approaches, scheduling procedures, and other joint efforts.

When a major buyer tells a smaller supplier that they ought to meet with you and consider your help so as to be congruent with the buyer's, you're going to get a very careful hearing. Moreover, don't forget that suppliers have their own vendors. You can work right down this supply chain until you reach a point of diminishing returns.

Most of us talk about the "customer's customer," but we don't follow our own advice. And remember that any one client might have dozens of major suppliers, so the leveraging effect is tremendous.

Action Step: Make a list of every active client over the past two years, and ask every buyer within each one for a list of those suppliers who might profit from your work. You should also make this a part of the discussion with every new client, every time.

11. Developing a Memorable Brand Phrase

One of my favorite brand names is The Telephone Doctor™, which is a firm founded and run by Nancy Friedman. I like it because it's so easy to say, "Get me The Telephone Doctor" or "Have you tried The Telephone Doctor?"[2]

---

2. See the second book in this series, *How to Establish a Unique Brand in the Consulting Profession,* for a detailed discussion of brand strategies.

> If you want prospective buyers to call you on their own volition, then give them something to call you.

One of the best sources of all for new business acquisition—and very timely for successful consultants—is to establish the "pull" of a successful brand and memorable brand name. A large part of McKinsey's success for a long time was due to the "Get me McKinsey" factor, almost irrespective of the nature of their work. Purchasing managers couldn't get fired for buying from IBM, and executives couldn't get dumped by the board for using McKinsey for their strategy work.

What kind of "hook" are you creating—based on your work, experience, and success—to enable people to quickly identify and call you?

A few years ago someone called me "the rock star of consulting." I was quite pleased. "Did I give you a new name?" she asked. "Well, that and a new source of income," I told her.

Action Step: Find a consultant, naming expert, coach, or trusted advisor, and establish two or three "brands" if you don't yet have them. Incorporate them into your website, print materials, speeches, networking, and so forth. If you're not sure of your brand strength, ask your best clients.

12. Selling to Your Suppliers

We all buy supplies, office equipment, design services, airline tickets, and a myriad of other things we take for granted in the running of our practices. But how often do we examine those often long-term relationships in terms of potential business?

You don't want to sell to your local print shop, but can the proprietor introduce you to the executives of Kinko's? If you're a good customer at Staples, can the manager recommend you to someone as a speaker for the annual management meeting? Your travel agent may have made some very nice commissions from your business over the years, and may be a part of one of the giant chains.

You've probably developed some excellent relationships with local vendors (whom I always advocate you pay first and quickly), and your business has been counted on in their own forecasts. You don't want to sell to them, but why not simply ask a small favor and get at least a name (and probably an endorsement) at the corporate level? The local Northwest Insurance broker, with a twenty-person staff, was able to place me as a keynote speaker at a major conference where I was seated next to the CEO.

Are you networking and seeking referrals among your own suppliers?

Action Step: Determine whom you've done the most business with, consistently, at the local level. Go to each of your contacts in these suppliers and ask for the appropriate party at the corporate level who would be interested in your work, and request an introduction. You'll find that you'll get one or more names at least 80 percent of the time.

BEST PRACTICES

Personal networking by far is the most effective for me. As an internal employee—one who hired consultants—I always trusted relationships first. If a consultant came through a good friend or someone very credible to me, I returned the call.

As an independent consultant myself, I have found that my business has grown rapidly through my network of relationships—generating bountiful referrals in many directions. An example: I was employed by one large company for twenty years. As people with whom I have relationships leave this company and go to other companies, they've taken me with them. It's been a huge source of expanded opportunity for me.

—Andrea C. Zintz, Ph.D., Andrea Zintz and Associates, LLC

THE FOURTH FOUR

13. Infiltrating Trade Associations

Trade associations provide tremendous visibility and contacts. Many allow membership to anyone interested (in other words, you don't have to be an active professional in the industry) and others provide "associate" memberships. Then there are the consulting, speaking, facilitation, coaching, and related professional associations, as well.

In any trade association, you can acquire prospects by engaging in the these types of activities:

Become an officer
Head a highly visible committee (for example, programming or membership)
Speak at the conventions
Exhibit at the conventions
Network at meetings
Take an ad in the directory
Provide pro bono consulting help
Recruit new members
Sponsor key events
Write for the association publications
Work to earn a professional designation or honor
Offer to mentor colleagues

There is an inherent credibility in serving in a formal capacity in professional organizations. Usually, the volunteer help is so weak that it's easy to stand out in a crowd. There is virtually never a competitive slate of board candidates, for example, so it's easy to serve with distinction.

Trade and professional organizations provide visibility to buyers, recommenders, and colleagues in the field who may refer you to business they can't handle. At this stage of your career, it's also an opportunity to "pay back."

Action Step: Join one or two professional associations with high potential and work to become very active (rather than join a dozen and remain inactive). Aside from all of the above, these can also be sources for lifelong learning in a profession that is otherwise quite lonely at times.

14. Obtaining a Profound Endorsement

When President Ronald Reagan mentioned that he was reading a terrific book called *The Hunt for Red October*, he didn't simply create a bestseller, he created a Tom Clancy industry. That was a profound endorsement!

We don't necessarily need an endorsement from a national figure or a celebrity. But we can do wonders when someone well-known in a particular field cites us favorably. We tend to do this normally, in our references and testimonials. When I tell a financial institution that I've worked with The Federal Reserve Bank, or an auto dealer that I've consulted with Mercedes-Benz, the conversation takes a decidedly upbeat turn.

Look for those few, key individuals who are well-known *among your prospect universe* and seek out ways to gain their endorsement or at least mention. It may be as simple as obtaining an introduction, or as difficult as finding some way to work together. Nevertheless, one positive word from a highly respected figure can short-cut your marketing process and generate new business immediately.

Action Step: Identify two markets or industries (or even geographies) that would constitute a new source of business acquisition, and determine who the most influential authorities are in those areas. Then generate a plan to gain their endorsement. Use the "six degrees of separation" approach: If you network assiduously, you are bound to find someone who knows someone who knows someone.

> No one is "unmeetable." If you persist and network diligently, you will eventually turn up a connection and perhaps an introduction. If you don't ask, however, you'll never meet anyone.

15. Writing The Book

This one seems obvious, but too few consultants pursue it because they think it's a field best left to the academics or that writing a book is akin to root canal work.

I know of no greater single credibility source than a commercially published book. At this stage of your career, there is really little excuse for *not* writing one. Simply follow this procedure:

A. Ask yourself whom you want to impress (which buyers).
B. Ask yourself what their greatest need is (their "trigger").
C. Ask yourself which of your competencies and experiences best meet the needs (your leverage).
D. Create a theme and ten chapter headings.
E. Write one chapter and two paragraphs about all other chapters.
F. Create a brief market analysis, comparing your proposed book to those already written on similar subjects.
G. Explain your uniqueness, credentials, marketing clout, and other supporting elements.
H. Get thee to an acquisitions editor or literary agent.

If you write only one page a day, you'll have a book in about nine months. If you follow the proposal outline above, you'll have something to show an editor or agent in thirty days. What's stopping you?

I have gained millions of dollars in consulting business from my books, far dwarfing the royalties and advances. The very words you're reading are going to earn me still more.

Action Step: Plan steps "A" to "H" above on your calendar, and get moving. Business books don't have to be scientifically tight, nor read like *The Grapes of Wrath*. They just have to use your experience and ideas to help people.

16. Getting a Referral Every Time

When I was young and newly married, an insurance agent named Hal Mapes sold me a small policy. He'd visit me once a quarter, and every time asked me for three names he could call. He literally wouldn't leave my house without those three names.

I figure that Hal probably had two hundred customers, so he was getting about 2,400 leads a year (twelve a year from each of us). If his close rate was even 5 percent, that represented 120 new policies at an average commission of at east $5,000 in the first year, or $600,000 annually, not counting other sources of business or a higher close rate.

Consultants are notoriously poor—at every stage of their careers—in obtaining referrals. The fact is, the more quality referrals received, even with a low close rate, the more likely that your business will grow exponentially. And when can you best expect the highest quality referrals? When you're successful and have solid relationships, that's when.

Action Step: Every single day, ask every client and prospect for three names of people who could benefit from your work. Do not take "no" for an answer. If you do this religiously, you will improve your business acquisition at virtually no cost.

FROM MY TIME IN THE TRENCHES

Even as successful veterans, we can find a multitude of ways to increase our business acquisition sources. I've explored only a few of my favorites here. But, as a check list, how many of these are you engaged in at the moment?

1. Partnering with professional colleagues
2. Harvesting low-hanging fruit
3. Using the Internet in reverse
4. Becoming the "middle man"
5. Publishing "unpromotional" articles
6. Serving the cause for free
7. Taking global vacations
8. Writing on the op-ed page
9. Franchising the talent
10. Pursuing your clients' vendors
11. Developing a memorable brand phrase
12. Selling to your suppliers
13. Infiltrating trade associations
14. Obtaining a profound endorsement
15. Writing The Book
16. Getting a referral every time

CHAPTER 6

Winning Friends and Influencing People

How to Build Support from Those Who Loathe Your Arrival

hen I was much younger, I used to hate the sales process, mainly because I saw it as basically adversarial. I thought that I had to convince someone to do something he or she didn't want to do, *rather than* provide help to someone who needs it. In every single transaction with a prospect, *some sale is going to be made.* The only question is whether you will convince the prospect that you can help him or her, or the prospect will convince you that you cannot.

It's that simple.

I significantly boosted my product sales and other passive income (which keeps me off airplanes and out of hotels) when I philosophically repositioned those products and services as remote help for my clients. We're reluctant to "peddle a book," for example, because we feel like encyclopedia salespeople. But I'm not reluctant at all to provide highly cost-efficient methods to continue the learning and improvement that my consulting and speaking has begun.

So the first step is philosophical: Do you see the "sales" process as adversarial, requiring the conquest of an opposing position? Or do you see it as supportive and helping, assisting the prospect in improving his or her condition? The second step is to understand that there are only three ways to change human behavior—your prospect's behavior—and two of them do not work:

Power. When you attempt to threaten someone, you might achieve brief movement, but you won't gain commitment. The sales techniques that attempt to scare people into acting ("You can't afford not to do this!") simply entrench people who are resistant to change.

Normative Pressure. This is peer pressure ("Don't be left out of this trend!"), which causes mass stampedes but little long-term enthusiasm. These tactics simply implore people to do what the competition has done (which is why so many lemming-like quality programs have failed).

Rational Self-Interest. Appeals to rational self-interest are the only tactics that ensure motivation, not merely movement. In this case the client understands just how important your help is *in improving his condition.* This is why sales can't be adversarial, but only mutually supportive.

If you revel in adversarial relationships, go into wrestling or the law. The buyer and the consultant are not on different sides. They should both want to improve the lot of the former.

PROVIDING VALUE EARLY AND FOR FREE

One of the great myths of the consulting profession is that we should not give anything away for free. After all, if we gave it away, then what would the client pay for?

The fact is that the best way to sell your ability to help is, well, *to help!* The philosophy that you want to create is, "If I'm getting this much help for free from this person, how much better off would I be if I actually hired him?" You obviously can't provide in-depth solutions or recommendations, but that's because you don't know enough yet and shouldn't be pretentious. But you can provide observations, experiences from elsewhere (which is why, supposedly, you're there to begin with), questions, and ideas, which gives the prospect two impressions:

1. There are some alternatives available that perhaps his or her own organization (or other consultants) haven't considered.
2. You are one smart person.

"Free" help with a prospect is the equivalent of your "loss leader"—you're luring the prospect into the store so that the more expensive merchandise can be purchased.

When a prospect says, "We never looked at it that way before," or "That's a novel approach for us," or "I wouldn't mind giving that a try here," you know that the only thing left for you is not to blow it. And bear in mind that this relationship building and value creation is prior to anyone talking about fees.

Who Could Make This Up?

A colleague named Jack asked me for help. He had the opportunity to address the top twenty-four people of Michelin North America, and he desperately wanted the presentation to lead to business. He had prepared the following form for each member of the group to sign:

> You are about to hear the ideas of Jack on productivity and performance. By signing this, you agree that these proprietary approaches may not be used unless Jack is engaged by Michelin for a project.

"What do you think?" he asked me.

"Well," I said, "why not just cut to the chase, stand up after you're introduced, and say, 'Good morning, I'm Jack, and I don't trust any single one of you.'?"

—AW

I'm convinced that providing value very early in the relationship cements the relationship and, ironically, leads to higher fees and larger initial projects. This approach is somewhat counterintuitive, and it's inherently uncomfortable for experienced consultants, who are often much more accustomed to being called in based on word of mouth and to devoting a great deal of time to reaffirming how good they are and how sound their approaches are.

> The sooner we begin providing value to a prospect, the sooner that the conversation focuses on their benefit, their improvement, and the value they derive. That means that costs, fees, and other discomfort become subordinate to their well-being.

The Ultimate Consultant should meet a new prospect with the philosophy and expressed attitude of finding the fastest and most effective method of helping that prospect. The *basic assumption* should be that you've obviously been asked to be there because you can be of help, and the only real issue is to determine how that should be manifest.

So don't try to "sell" anyone, whether at an initial meeting or at follow-up sessions. Instead provide value. And fight the conventional wisdom that you should carefully prepare to address specific content and issues in the prospect's industry or organization. *Your basic value is that you can bring approaches, experiences, and wisdom for a variety of organizations and, one hopes, an assortment of industries. Don't undercut your own advantage by appearing as simply another potential employee!* When Mercedes-Benz told me I knew nothing of the auto industry, I told them that that was exactly the point: They had automotive experts falling out of the rafters and lying in the halls, but they had no one like me who could share with them how Merck, Hewlett-Packard, and Chase were dealing with analogous issues.

As veteran, successful consultants, we can make such arguments and comparisons. To refuse or fail to do so is simply negligent—and inexcusably undermines your abilities to win friends and influence buyers.

BUILDING MOMENTUM AMONG KEY ADVISORS

The sales process is seldom scripted or perfect, so your route to and dealings with the buyer will often be littered with advisors, assistants, subordinates, gatekeepers, and assorted hangers-on. There are times, alas, when some of these people have to be taken seriously.

Many buyers do rely on advice and counsel from others, and your appeal to and relationships with them may decide the deal, especially when there is competition for the project. In my experience, there are three kinds of people surrounding the decision maker:

> *Close Counselors.* These are usually either direct reports or long-time, trusted friends to whom the buyer turns for what he or she considers to be unadulterated and objective feedback. They seldom generate the alternative (you), but they often critique and comment on it. Close counselors may be peers, people in other departments, and even non-company acquaintances.
>
> *Vetoes.* Vetoes are people whose affirmation isn't necessarily needed, but who can effectively deep-six an initiative through the threat of non-support. These are usually informal leaders or entrenched subordinates with loyal followings. Vetoes can include union leaders, high-producing salespeople, a tough financial officer who may poke around the project, and so on. These are people who can't force a "yes" but can generate a "no."

The king is usually surrounded by a court. Sometimes you can simply walk the red carpet and engage the king, and sometimes you must charm the lords and ladies in waiting.

> *Stumbling Blocks.* These are the folks whom you keep tripping over as you try to walk to and from the buyer. They are sometimes required (secretaries, assistants) and sometimes superfluous (staff people, displaced poor performers), but almost always in the way. The major challenge with stumbling blocks is, well, not to stumble over them.

Here are some questions you can quickly use to determine with whom you are interacting. They are as relevant on a first meeting as on follow-up calls, and they will greatly help with the management of your sales time. (Close Counselor = CC; Veto = V; Stumbling Block = SB)

Ten Questions to Determine Advisors' Roles
1. Does the buyer personally invite these people to meetings? (CC)
2. Does the buyer cite the people in terms of their suggestions and concerns? (CC)
3. Does the buyer ask you to debrief with these people and consider their suggestions? (CC)
4. Does the buyer encourage other people to contact you independently, and do they do so? (CC)
5. Does the buyer ask your counsel and solicit strategy on how to "bring certain people on board"? (V)
6. Does the buyer say things like, "We'll have to reposition this if it's going to be digested"? (V)
7. Does the buyer cite people in association with other projects that have been derailed or otherwise undermined? (V)
8. Does the buyer take pleasure in "putting something over" on someone or in forcing a change that "has been resisted over there for too long"? (V)
9. Does the buyer never mention the person's name or acknowledge his or her role? (SB)
10. Does the buyer act contemptuously or say, "Leave them to me"? (SB)

By performing this quick "triage" (and you should be able to identify anyone by your second or third interaction) you'll be able to focus your efforts and energy in influencing the people surrounding the buyer:

Stumbling Blocks. Ignore them. Don't be impolite, particularly with those assistants and aides whom you might see regularly, but don't spend a lot of time massaging the relationship.[1] If you are rude or impolite, you're

---

1. By the way, it's largely a myth that a secretary can control everything from a boss's calendar to his or her choice of consultants. So keep your flowers and chocolates for your immediate family. Besides, most secretaries have heard it all before and you're hardly the first to think you can sneak in the side door.

indeed going to trip over them. Treat them well, but move toward the objective.

Vetoes. Never approach vetoes without a strategy, and preferably one put together with the buyer and the close counselors. You need a cultural, historical, and contextual reference base to truly understand the potential animosity of these people. And don't forget that usually one strong "no" is all that's needed—there is seldom a second chance. So go slow, and understand that the buyer wants to romance, circumvent, or blow up these people as much as you do.

One of the greatest inefficiencies in the sales process is caused by according equal time and respect to everyone we meet. Even after the buyer, there are degrees of importance. A duke is always more important than the dog warden.

Close Counselors. Romance them, but don't mistake them for the buyer. (They cannot say "yes" and cannot sign the check.) Ask the buyer—and this is key—about the extent to which he or she desires these people, by name, to be involved (for example, copying them on email, expecting them at meetings, providing them with copies of the proposal, and so forth). Work with the buyer to understand the need for and degree of their involvement. And *always* copy the buyer and inform the buyer about your dealings with the close counselors. More than one sale has been lost when the consultant has forfeited the relationship with the buyer to focus on the counselors.

Understand with whom you are dealing and adjust your responses accordingly. This is not harsh, not unethical, not abusive. It is smart selling. The friend you want to win is the buyer, and the people you want to influence are those who can help you win that important friend.

DEALING WITH COMMITTEES

Committees are such a ubiquitous fact of life that I think we need to spend some dedicated time on them. We've all heard "The committee will be evaluating the

The One That Got Away

We had been working with the Bell Telephone Companies back when they were still affiliated with AT&T (prior to the 1984 decree). Through those contacts we became aware of a need for an information retrieval system that could be satisfied by a scaled-down version of a directory assistance system that we were already selling to Michigan Bell and NYNEX.

The application was to be used by C&P telephone initially, and we used our relationship with C&P to formulate our offering. As luck would have it, AT&T saw the applicability of this type of system across all of the Bell companies and entered into the picture just prior to the issuance of the RFP and took responsibility for the entire procurement process. We had what we believed to be contacts within AT&T and briefed them on our capabilities before the RFP came out—after which no additional direct contact was permitted until the proposals were submitted.

Part of the evaluation process required all bidders to conduct live trials of their systems at one of the Bell companies. We tested ours at C&P, and it was a resounding success that met all of the requirements of the specification and proved its return on investment for the user. In addition, we learned that our bid price was 16 percent lower than the next-nearest competitor.

Wow! All we had to do was wait for the order to come in.

About two weeks before the previously announced due date for a formal selection, we received some additional questions from AT&T as to how we

various options" and "The committee will be making the recommendation" and "The committee has delayed the decision."

Here's some honest scoop on committees:

- Committees are *never* decision-making bodies for consulting services, no matter what you're told or led to believe. Committees are *recommending* bodies. They have no discrete budgets. They are often composed of people who are potential "vetoes," simply to ensure they've had a "voice" in the choice of resources.

could expand the system to embrace some other capabilities. Our design was geared to running a specific application as a means of getting the performance demonstrated in the trial and keeping the cost low. However, we did find a way of addressing the requested enhancement, but it did complicate the application. We briefed this response to the AT&T people and they seemed satisfied, but we did not have as good a relationship with them as with the C&P folks.

After another two weeks, the inevitable news came that the contract had been awarded to a competitor in Colorado. It turns out that they were a three-person company who were former employees of AT&T. Their solution was to add this application to a mainframe system that they had worked on when previously employed by AT&T, and the genesis of the original RFP requirement lost its identity and became embedded in an unrecognizable program running who knows what other applications.

In retrospect, there were several lessons learned. Perhaps the biggest was that we just didn't know the economic buyer nearly as well when the requirement responsibility was taken over by AT&T. Clearly, the importance of this application was not seen the same way by AT&T as it was by the Operator Services people at each of the Bell companies. We also underestimated the competition and disregarded the ultimate winner as an also-ran because of their size and prior experience.

—Joe Boschi, President, Buckhorn Consulting Group

Committees are effective in inverse proportion to their size. A committee of over ten people tends to be dysfunctional and has the consciousness of a jellyfish—they float with the tide and winds and compete with plankton. A committee of fewer than six people tends to act with some direction and has the consciousness of a trained seal—it can perform certain activities if duly fed and housed.

> If you are "stuck" in a committee, it's because you have entered into a collusion with that body. When you step in gum, it will eventually wear itself off your shoe, but it might take miles and days. You're better off scraping off the gum on a curb or buying a new pair of shoes.

There is always a power source on a committee. All members are not created equal. There is what you might call a "committee influencer." This is the person, by dint of formal or informal position or merely loudest voice, who will most bend, cajole, and imprint those around the table.

Committees contain infighting. Do not take sides or attempt to align yourself with the presumed power block. You can't possibly understand the backstage maneuvering taking place. Do not allow yourself to be used by one side against the other.

Committees comprise individuals. There is no law or ethical imperative that says you cannot establish relationships with key members individually to educate yourself (and them) better.

Committees are boring. Sometimes the most powerful and influential members will not attend the meetings. If you must deal with a committee, insist on receiving the names and contact points for all members, and ingratiate yourself to those whom you do not meet at the sessions.

The larger the committee, the more loose lips. Ask the members in general or individually how the decision will really be made, who the economic buyer actually is, and what will constitute the best chances of success. Someone, somewhere, at some point, will spill the beans.

You can take a shortcut with most committees by proving that you're a "sole source"[2] supplier. By that I mean that you provide some unique approach, service, expertise, and/or experience that no one else they talk to can possibly match. The easiest and surest route to "sole source": If you have a commercially published book related by topic to the project under

---

2. This is a technique I've long used with government requests for proposals (RFPs) to escape the competitive bidding process. It's legal and often actually preferred by the buyers.

discussion, you are virtually automatically a sole source (no one else has written that book).

Appeal to the committee on a different basis than your competitors will. Don't be the twelfth person through the door with a PowerPoint™ presentation or slick brochures or templates. I once closed a sale in a competitive process by showing up with precisely nothing and asking a series of pointed questions of the evaluators. Every person in that room remembered my different approach to the session.

Finally, avoid committees by circumventing, evading, and charging through them. At best they slow up the buying process and, at worst, serve only as "deselection" points. Find the true buyer and proceed to that person. Tell the buyer that you deal as a partner with the decision maker, and that you don't work through committees because, in your experience, that isn't how collaborative relationships are explored and built. You may just get the work. Of course, you may also get thrown out, but you're probably just getting the bad news a lot quicker and with less frustration.

I don't believe that committees are a part of the natural process of acquiring business. Whether you decide to deal with them or not will be enabling or disabling behavior. It's really a philosophic choice.

When you tell the buyer that you don't deal with committees, but rather only with decision makers, also stress that in your past projects you've always advised clients to abandon committees in favor of more direct leadership. Explain to the buyer that committees are no more skilled at selecting consultants to work in partnership with him or her than they would be to select the buyer's car or legal advisor. It must be a personal decision on both your parts.

OVERCOMING "THREAT" FACTORS

There are various true land mines and snipers that can imperil your journey toward winning friends and influencing people. They are worse in some organizations than others, but it's rare not to encounter any at all. "Threat" factors are those organizational, cultural, and environmental realities that advertently or inadvertently serve to prevent you from reaching and establishing a relationship with the economic buyer.

Committees are structural roadblocks, and have been discussed above. But here are some of the additional obvious and non-obvious threat factors that may derail your efforts to pull into the station:

Unions. There are many situations in which unions have a visceral hatred of consultants, with the understandable reason that every prior consultant has recommended a reduction in the work force as the panacea. Sometimes, in terrible labor/management climates, the union will simply oppose anything management seeks to do, especially if it involves spending money. This is a very serious potential obstacle.

Action: First, don't let the union issue overwhelm the relationship building. Establish trust with the buyer and elicit the major issues to be improved, irrespective of the union. Then discuss potential approaches. Finally, when you have conceptual agreement with the buyer on the objectives and the methodologies that might make sense, create a strategy for embracing the union (for example, co-opt key formal and informal leaders) or avoiding trouble (for example, begin in non-union areas of the operation).

Fatal: Never begin by focusing on the union issue, nor treat it as the issue. That will immediately cast you as both a management shill (from the union perspective) and helpless (from management's perspective).

Human Resources. If HR departments were stronger and more aggressive, there would be much less work for consultants. But that's not a condition that will arise any time within our lifetimes. Some HR departments will welcome you with open arms and say, "Thank goodness that you're here. Now that they're paying you a fortune, they'll finally believe what we've been telling them for free for years!" More often, however, HR will be threatened and attempt to undermine the project beginning because of fears that blame will alight on their desks.

A few times, when I was unable to make direct contact with a prospect, I sent a gift with my sales letter. I tied the letter to the gift. To be specific, once I sent a large cheese and opened the letter with "Be a big cheese." Another time I sent a set of nested baskets, with a message in each basket.

The final basket had chocolates in it, and my closing message said that our services could lead to "sweet success." In both cases, when I followed up with a phone call, I got through.

—Maria Thomson, Managing Principal,
Thomson Management Solutions, Inc.

Action: Never allow yourself to be delegated to the human resources function to "get background" or "get a feel for our people." Stress that you're happy to collaborate with them as appropriate on the implementation, but that the strategy and tactics must be designed and agreed on by the buyer and you. In fact, it's never risky to point out that the reason things have progressed to where they are might be because of the HR department, and you'd rather remain independent for both objectivity and credibility purposes until you can learn more about the situation.

Fatal: If you allow a project to become an "HR project," you will immediately lose credibility with the greater organization, lose the close partnership needed with the economic buyer, and lose your ability to function independently and, perhaps, critically of HR.

Your job is not to make people love you. Your job is to improve your client's condition. You confuse those two objectives only at your own peril. Only the buyer can rehire you. The employees cannot.

Prevailing Politics. Every organization is political. The question is whether or not the politics are dysfunctional and whether or not they threaten the project. You will know this early when you hear things such as, "Sales will not support this because they think that operations takes too much of the budget" or "R&D is a problem because the VP hates our VP." Don't take on assignments that are what I call "grudge projects": There is no real client condition to be improved, but rather an act of vengeance, or put-down, or retribution to be enacted.

Action: Always remain centered on observable behavior and objective fact. Don't go along with "We'll have to fool R&D on this," but instead state "I'll have to talk to the R&D vice president myself to understand his position." Focus on the organizational performance to be improved and not on one party benefiting *at the expense of another party.* Explain to your buyer that you are most effective for him or her by taking the sincere role of objective third party and not being seen as someone's shill.

Fatal: Allowing yourself to immediately be seen as a "wedge" or "weapon" being employed to elevate one person or department at the expense of another. This will immediately close doors and shut down cooperation. Never, ever simply accept a buyer's version of another's motives or description of his or her behavior. Take it under advisement, but check it out yourself.

Fishing Expeditions. Some organizations will invite you in with great fanfare and camaraderie only to try to learn what you would do, how you would do it, and how much it would cost. While I do believe in giving value away for free and early in the sales process, I also believe it should be done to whet the buyer's appetite, not to complete the plans for the project before money has changed hands! I call these "fishing expeditions" because they are a method that some individuals employ to find out what they don't know at the consultant's expense.

Action: Limit your early discussions to the buyer, not to large groups. Emphasize that you're providing some tentative ideas, but that a more detailed analysis of the situation is required. Impress on the buyer the uniqueness that you bring in experience, approaches, and talents, so that it's apparent that other parties could not simply take your ideas and run with them. Provide macro and strategic approaches, not micro and tactical ones.

Fatal: Providing a proposal so detailed and technical that explicit steps and methodologies are outlined that do not require your specific skill and expertise to implement. These overly detailed documents—utterly unnecessary in order to close a sale with an economic buyer—are often used either as a template for internal resources or as a guide to other external consultants who submit lower fees.

> The key focus must be on WHAT is to be accomplished rather than HOW you will do it. The client is the expert on health care, or automobiles, or photography. You are the expert on consulting. You shouldn't tell the client how to build brake linings, and the client shouldn't tell you how to sample the employee population. Keep your precise tactical plans to yourself.

Dwindling Funds. Sometimes when you're called in for remedial work, or because of a "surprise" development, there will be insufficient funds to do the job well. The client might tell you that "More will be forthcoming" or that "We'll need to spread this over two fiscal years" or that "If we make a strong enough first impression the president will have to allocate more funds." Don't believe it for a minute. This is where consultants become entrapped in the La Brea Tar Pits of organizational evolution. Only the bones eventually emerge.

Action: Establish your fee for your various options in your proposal, and demand at least a 50 percent deposit. Demand the other 50 percent in a reasonable amount of time (forty-five or sixty days), but do not wait until the project is over. This is not the contingency fee business, where the lawyers must pray for the class action suit to reward their clients handsomely so that they can take 40 percent of it. A client's inability or unwillingness to pay at the beginning does not indicate prudence, *it indicates an inability and/or unwillingness to pay at any time whatsoever.* If you're truly worth it in terms of the value you deliver (the improved condition), then this should never be an issue.

Fatal: Accepting work with a promise for later payment, and then accepting the client's word that "If we do just a little more we can free up the dollars we need." Try telling that to your bank at mortgage payment time. If the client doesn't provide a sizeable deposit, don't start work. If the client fails to meet a payment deadline during the project, stop work. It's really that simple.

BEST PRACTICES

I was a representative for a large silicone manufacturing company. For this one particular prospect representing a $50K+ annual sales order, I hand-delivered several product samples many times over a three-month period, as well as product data, literature, and MSDS sheets. During three visits to the prospect's facility, I'd noticed some of my samples remained unopened.

When I asked him about it, he would only say, "We are still evaluating." Finally, after calling him to set up the appointment, he told me he had come to a decision. He was going with my competition. With nothing to lose, I resorted to my "kick over the table" strategy. In a sense, I was holding a pair of deuces while my competition apparently had a full house, leaving me no other alternative but to kick over the table.

I began berating the prospect, accusing him of leading me on for three months and not giving our products a fair and honest shot. That I did everything he had asked of me and more. That in spite of my efforts, I bet I could walk into his plant right now and find my samples never tried and still unopened. I could see him turning red in the face with anger and stating something to the effect that I had a lot of nerve. I told him I felt he had more nerve than I did for not being fair with either me or the products. That unless he did give us a fair shot, he'd be stuck with the competition's product with no offset or backup should they ever have a production problem with their material, which in turn could cause him to shut down his own production line.

He caved. He agreed to test our products fairly, and in the end, the competition and I split the $50K in annual sales.

—Jim Altfeld, President, Altfeld, Inc.

Scope Creep. This is the classic consulting problem, but it is caused at the outset, not during a project. It is a function of the business acquisition process. The client leaves things so open-ended, and dangles such inviting money, that the consultant doesn't take pains to specify the exact outcomes and precise improvement desired. Consequently, with this "blank check," the buyer continues to demand more and more help in more and more areas until the project becomes vastly unprofitable, despite the original fees.

Action: Focus on specific objectives, measures, and improvement (value) during the relationship-building stage. Gain conceptual agreement on these parameters; then specify them all in your written proposal. Do not accept "Let's just begin and we'll work out the details as we go along." As attractive as that sounds, it's deadly.

Fatal: Accepting an assignment without clear objectives and, therefore, parameters for your work. If someone simply wants access to your "smarts," use a retainer arrangement instead.[3]

> Money that looks too easy at the outset usually is. Flaky deals tend to get flakier and tight deals tend to remain tight. This is all established before anyone signs off on a proposal.

FROM MY TIME IN THE TRENCHES

Consulting services have to be marketed and sold. This is a marketing business, make no mistake about it. The key, however, to generating early and strong relationships is in providing value, not withholding ideas out of fear of theft. The higher level the buyer, the safer this is.

There are usually key advisors as well as non-key players around the buyer. Learn to discriminate among those who can help, those who can hurt, and those who don't matter, and apportion your time and energy accordingly. Try not to deal with committees at all but, if you must, use some tactics to gain yourself the maximum leverage and influence with the members.

---

3. See my earlier book in The Ultimate Consultant Series, *Value-Based Fees: How to Charge for Your Value and Get What You're Worth* (Jossey-Bass/Pfeiffer, 2002).

Every new business environment and culture contains inherent threats to your immediate acquisition of business and/or longer-term successful delivery of that business. Learn to identify them early in order to take effective preventive action. If you don't, the contingent action is usually painful and always a diminution of your profits.

The only critical person to influence is the economic buyer. In the end, if you identify that person and develop a strong relationship, you'll have the leverage and partnership needed to overcome almost any threat.

CHAPTER 7

Gaining Market Share from Others

Stealing Is Legal in the Sales Business

Consulting services, as far as I know, are not client consumables that are required every day like coffee, copy paper, and memo pads. There is a "closed market" for consulting in that a given client usually needs only one strategy consultancy, one sales improvement process, and one technology integration plan.

In fact, since it's relatively easy to extend and enlarge work within a client once a consultant has successfully implemented a project, and since that extension may well be to diverse areas of client need and consultant expertise, one can make the point that there is limited "market share" available in our business. Especially in plateaued or declining economies, the amount of potential consulting work is finite, so the ability to grow a business is often dependent on taking business that previously belonged to others.

To a great degree, this is counterintuitive. I've long preached, for instance, that there's a "discounting principle" involved, which states that a successful consultant maintaining a solid relationship with an economic buyer is extraordinarily difficult to displace because a newcomer to the scene can't possibly seek to replicate the relationship, the value it represents, and the shared successes from a standing start. In fact, the established consultant can charge higher fees than the consultant seeking to penetrate the client account and still hold a huge advantage.

In view of that tremendous strength, which accrues from carefully nurtured relationships, how does one improve one's business by enlarging his or her market share at the inevitable expense of others? *Make no mistake about this point: The reason that so many successful consultants find themselves plateaued and caught in the "success trap" is that they have never engaged in a strategy or mastered the skills to enlarge their market share by gaining client business from others.*

Unless you are growing, you are on the road to decline. All plateaus eventually erode. Unless you are taking market share from others, you are not growing significantly.

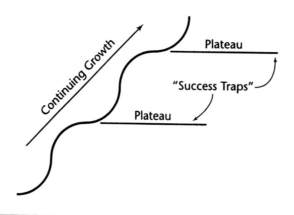

Figure 7.1. The Success Traps Resulting from Lack of Market Share Growth

How to Acquire Clients

Decline inevitably results from lack of growth due to the following inter-play of factors:

Revenues cease growing because one's existing market is saturated
One's existing market evaporates due to retirement of buyers, technologi-cal usurpation, relocation of facilities, and new competition
One's life style continues to improve and grow, but at a rate faster than rev-enue growth
Infrastructure and business expenses grow faster than revenues, particu-larly if one's strategy has been to build staff
As one concentrates marketing efforts in highly successful areas, potential buyers outside of those areas are ignored and one's reputation and brand become better and better known in fewer and fewer areas

Ultimate Consultants build on strength and momentum and seek new markets as their past successes enable them to make such investments. Let's take a look at how that's done.

HARVESTING "LOW HANGING FRUIT"

Low hanging fruit refers to those attractive items easiest to reach. The phrase has been around for a long time, but the power of the metaphor as a marketing tool struck me most powerfully while working with one of my high-tech clients in 2001 (see Who Could Make This Up? on page 115).

An important note: New consultants can use this particular principle to great advantage, since they have no current market share and need to steal someone else's. If you are hiring inexperienced staff, or if you are new to the profession and have the good sense to read this "advanced" book, this one sec-tion should be an even more essential aspect of your market strategy.

There are actually advantages in attempting to steal a rival's market share. There are normally quite a few resistance factors or "hurdles" that must be negotiated in order to convert a buyer who has not used consultants before. But in pursuing buyers who are already using other consultants, you have the advantage of having many of those resistance factors already overcome by the incumbent consulting firm.

> Pursuing buyers who are already inclined to use consulting services and, even better, are accustomed to paying significant fees for them is an entirely rational and intelligent strategy.

"Low hanging fruit," therefore, constitutes prospective organizations that have the following characteristics:

Frequent Use of Consultants. There are many organizations that make no bones about utilizing consulting help. You can learn about them by networking at trade association meetings, reading industry publications such as *Consultants News* and *C2M (Consulting to Management)*, and by reading *The Wall Street Journal, Business Week, Inc., Forbes, Fortune, Fortune Small Business*, and similar sources. Most consulting firms will list their clients somewhere in their literature or on their websites.

Use of a Variety of Consulting Firms. Even better are those firms that are not "married" to a single consulting firm. By talking to employees in Hewlett-Packard, for example, you'll find that the firm historically has used "big five" firms, large specialty firms, solo practitioners, moonlighting college professors, small training companies, and guest speakers.

Willingness to Pay High Fees in Return for High Value. Many firms fulfilling the first two characteristics will also be pecuniary—they will pay only by the hour and only miserly (almost always the case in technology consulting). Instead, you need those firms, no matter what your intended market, that have known that paying high fees to derive high return simply represents intelligent investment.

Clearly Identifiable Buyers and Buying Points. To continue to "short cut" the process, truly low hanging fruit will be identifiable by a clear purchase point. In a smaller business it may be the owner or CEO, in a larger organization the vice president of sales or general manager of retail services. You must be able to spot the buyer—through networking, newspaper articles, industry sources, or insider tips—and not waste time working your way through the gatekeepers (who

How to Acquire Clients

will be even more disinclined to help if there is already an established consulting presence favored by their superiors).

An Acceptance of Need. In more traditional business acquisition, we often have to establish a need first (marketing) and then convince the buyer that we have the answer to that need (selling). In the pursuit of low hanging fruit, we want to focus on those prospects who admit to the need (although we may still be able to enlarge it after establishing a relationship). Highest prospects with these traits are those stipulating that they need to cut costs, improve sales, increase public image, digest an acquisition, reverse a misfortune, and so on.

Who Could Make This Up?

I was asked to work with the internal (telemarketing) sales force of a high-tech firm selling Internet advertising. This was a simple business during the roaring Nineties market, but became very tough—and extraordinarily competitive—once high tech plunged a couple of years ago.

The salespeople were struggling. The old line "brick and mortar" firms didn't believe in web advertising (another very high hurdle to be overcome), and the Internet firms were either saturated or disappearing.

As a consultant, I'm skilled in looking for distinctions. And I found an outstanding one: A salesman named Paul Serino was selling like a crazy person. In fact, he had earned over a third of a million dollars sitting in the same area where everyone else was struggling to make $50,000. Being no fool, I asked him just what the heck he was doing.

"Low hanging fruit," he said, as if that explained it all. With prompting, he told me that it was silly to try to convince people to advertise on the Internet when there were so many people already convinced. He simply investigated who was advertising and where (easy enough to do by watching ads on the computer screen) and told those buyers that his company had better positioning and higher quality at competitive rates. He didn't try to sell on price, but sold against the existing need.

There was enough low hanging fruit to earn Paul's company several million dollars and him a nice living. Why strain to reach higher if the business is all around your head?

—AW

> Why take the risks of climbing up a tree when there is high quality fruit within reach at ground level? You don't need a ladder, don't need a partner, won't take a fall, and won't bruise the fruit. Are you looking up in anticipation rather than looking around in awareness?

Take a morning to determine what prospects fulfill *all* of my five characteristics, then devise a plan to reach them. The extent to which you travel from your current markets is a function of your own boldness and energy. I've worked for industries including automotive, banking, pharmaceutical, insurance, specialty chemical, real estate, newspapers, recreation, consulting, travel, and over two dozen others. Why haven't you?

CREATING HIGH VISIBILITY

If you want to steal business, you're going to need "instant credibility." You will not have the opportunity to build and nurture a relationship over a long term and hope for credibility growth through osmosis. You're going to need "presence." This is where a brand and/or personal name recognition are vital.[1]

While you are successful you can't stop your marketing. *While you are successful* you will have the greatest momentum and impact associated with your marketing. If you want to steal business, you need to gain visibility in areas other than the ones representing your current success.

Here are some techniques to gain high visibility in areas that you would like to penetrate at the expense of those already there:

Publish Outside Your Field

I've reached out to the executive recruiting profession and published an article on why that group is charging at rates far below the value being delivered. I have a monthly column on an Internet site for high-tech people. I've published

---

1. See my earlier book in this series, *How to Establish a Unique Brand in the Consulting Profession* (Jossey-Bass/Pfeiffer, 2001).

about value propositions in the franchise industry. The greatest downside is a rejection or two, which is negligible. The upside is the name recognition gained by new prospective buyers. When the time comes for you to pursue them actively, you can point to a body of work in their field and, perhaps, they might even know of you by repute. The "golden" road to rapidly gaining market share: a commercially published, well-reviewed book.

Speak Outside Your Field

There are thousands of meetings every week requiring speakers. There are few routes as rapid and direct to gain credibility in a new market as intelligently addressing a room full of potential buyers. You can always—always—take elements of your existing strengths and apply them to a new marketplace. I found that I was a huge hit at the American Grain and Feedlot Association and the National Fisheries Institute simply by helping them to understand their own lack of consumer awareness rather than attempting to help them raise cattle or harvest fish better, which they already know better than anyone. You are the "fresh air" that many industries need, too long accustomed to listening to the same old content experts.

> Start building recognition and visibility in new areas tomorrow. If you had begun a year ago, you'd probably have a larger market share right now than you do. Every day you delay, you also freeze your current market share.

Forge an Alliance That Is Synergistic

You're not going to forge an alliance with someone already doing well in that market for the purpose of him or her losing market share so that you can gain it! However, you can find others who stand to mutually gain by a foray into new territory. For example, if you wish to penetrate the recreation market, you may find a seminar provider who has never worked in that market but finds it equally attractive. The seminar firm can simply take its existing marketing savvy, you can simply take your existing expertise, and both of you can pursue workshops that will generate revenue for them and both revenue and recognition in the industry for you. This is a win/win/win proposition that can be very effective in penetrating new markets.

BEST PRACTICES

Business Card Engagement: (1) Exchanging business cards at the beginning of the interaction allows the consultant/sales professional the power in remembering the other person's name by way of a simple glance at the card. Most people—immediately after shaking hands in the greeting stage of meeting someone for the first time—almost instantly forget that person's name.

(2) As you talk with the prospect and focus on the needs analysis of that person, you can use the reverse side of your own business card, label it with the date, and write personal and specific solutions to the prospect's needs. While the prospect is almost surely going to discard all collateral materials given to them by a consultant, the business card now becomes a customized brochure and is seen as more personal and valuable and will be kept by the prospect or customer!

(3) After the meeting, take the person's business card and place reminder notes on the reverse and add some personal notes if necessary to help you to remember this new person after the fact.

(4) By actively using business cards this way, you can also measure how many interactions you are having. A growth-oriented consultant should be going through at least five hundred business cards a month!

—Jeffrey L. Magee, Ph.D., CMC, Founder/CEO,
JEFF MAGEE INTERNATIONAL, Inc.

The Ultimate Consultant has the following advantages, which accrue to those who have been uniquely successful:

Strong name recognition in certain fields
Publishing and/or interview history
Speaker and/or panelist experience

Strong references and testimonials

Media contacts

Comfort in sales situations and in dealing with economic buyers

Strong image and collateral materials

Financial resources to invest in additional marketing

Support people, subcontractors, reliable sources for help

The time to "steal" clients is when you don't need to. That means that ideally you should be building toward that end well in advance. Visibility is best gained through a body of work over a prolonged period. Thus, the "steal" is gradual and relentless, not a sudden storm of the castle that is easily repelled.

At least 20 percent of the marketing efforts of a successful consultant should be geared toward markets he or she wants to penetrate in another year, business he or she wants to "steal" in the mid-term future, and recognition he or she wants to gain later in one's career. And that figure may well be too low to sustain truly dramatic growth.

Thus far we've discussed the proactive and assertive techniques of pursuing "low hanging fruit" and deliberately generating higher visibility in high potential new areas in order to gain market share at someone else's expense. However, there is another quite favorable phenomenon that you can't engender. That occurs when the existing, entrenched consultant blows it.

WAITING FOR SOMEONE ELSE'S BAD NEWS

All of us have failed. If we hadn't, we wouldn't be as successful as we are today. I wasn't a philosophy major, but it seems to me logical to deduce:

You are an excellent consultant

All excellent consultants fail at times

Highly desirable and smart prospects will use excellent consultants

At some point, some of those excellent consultants will fail
Smart clients will then seek out other excellent consultants
You are an excellent consultant

Okay, it's not exactly Hegelian, but I think it's a sound point. Even entrenched consultants will get tossed at some point. If you still think that's far-fetched, here are the reasons in my experience of getting tossed myself:

1. The project failed because I took on more than was reasonable to accomplish and oversold the expectations to the buyer.
2. The project failed because I made a major error in assumptions, analysis, or implementation.
3. The buyer changed.
4. Disgruntled subordinates sabotaged the results or undermined the perceptions of my progress.
5. The economy changed and caused a downturn in the client's industry.
6. The competition scooped the client with new technology or approaches.
7. More important priorities dwarfed the original importance of the project.
8. I delivered honest but damning news and the buyer preferred to shoot the messenger (this one revisits me periodically).
9. I was not sufficiently attached to the acknowledged results of the project.
10. An industry "fad" (such as reengineering) brainwashed the client into pursuing a route I was not able to provide or chose not to provide.

Every day, consultants get tossed out of work. In the vast majority of cases, that means work for some other consultant. The client does not go "cold turkey." Outside help is as addictive as controlled substances, but legal in most states.

This approach is a variation of "low hanging fruit," in that the prospect believes in consulting services and has hired consultants, preferably at high fees. The key here is what I call the "value campaign." Since timing is everything (you need to appear as an alternative when the client is seeking such an alternative), and you can't possibly predict when that time will precisely occur, you need to be "omnipresent."

Target those dozen or so high profile and potentially lucrative clients whom you would love to do business with but who are utilizing others in areas in which you would compete.[2] Then create your "value campaign" so that you are known as a resource *should the client decide he or she is in need of one.*

Value campaign features can include:

A Newsletter by Electronic or Hard Copy. But unlike a traditional marketing newsletter, this should be tightly focused on the targets you've identified. Hence, the need for a relatively few such targets. You might even customize the newsletter for each particular target, using precise examples, names, facts, and so on. The reader will not know this is a "narrowcast" but will assume that your newsletter speaks to the industry or subject area, yet is particularly pertinent for him or her.

Trade Association Leadership or Visibility. Become active in the prospect's major trade association and manage to serve on a committee or represent an initiative, which provides a reasonable excuse for a conversation, exchange of views, periodic contact, and so forth. Choose your visibility selectively, focusing on that high potential prospect as the key target.

Request the Use of the Target Organization in a Flattering Article or Interview. Find something about that prospect's organization that will fit with an article you're doing on a relevant topic. For example, they may have a higher retention rate than the industry average due to an innovative benefits program. Note that the article does not have to be (and perhaps should not be) in the area in which you want to penetrate.

Use the "Six Degrees of Separation" Approach.[3] Network to find a direct access to the key buyer and secure an introduction or referral. Your objective is not to

---

2. My assumption throughout is that your expertise would not be additional to that already hired, but would duplicate it, meaning one of you would have to go.

3. Originally a game that stipulated that any celebrity could be traced to actor Kevin Bacon in no more than six steps through mutual acquaintances, joint ventures, common movies, and so on.

uproot the existing consulting resource, since this approach assumes that the incumbent will be doing fine until the failure point. The objective is rather to be known to the buyer and within recall when that failure point occurs.

The "value campaign" differs from traditional marketing in that:

The focus is on a very few, high potential targets that currently utilize consulting services in your areas of expertise
The tactics are highly focused and even personalized to the particular profiles of that organization and that buyer
The emphasis is on a "brand awareness" so that you are within easy memory if the need to replace existing resources is suddenly required
You are striving for recognition and a "soft sell" and not an immediate relationship and specific intervention

> Because a "value campaign" has to be quite specific, choose your targets very selectively, but then be relentless in creating a favorable and "omnipresent" recognition factor.

The value of a rigorous and disciplined campaign against the possibility of the other guy failing is that the relationship building will be accelerated. Clients seeking replacements usually don't have the residual talents to compensate for the loss of the consultant, their culture accommodates outside intervention, and the buyer has probably come to rely on it. (Many buyers say their only "honest" feedback comes from external consultants.) Hence, the buyer is in somewhat of a hurry to replace the lost resource. If you've been successfully "hovering" in the background, the buyer might not have to look very far.

MORE TECHNIQUES TO TRESPASS ON OTHERS' PROPERTY

Effective consulting is about effective marketing, relationship building, and collaboration with an economic buyer. The consulting skills are the least of it, since

The Twilight Zone

The most unusual sales situation. One of my very successful clients asked me to coach his daughter, a hippie, to handle the advertising for his company. She was on drugs and not particularly interested in business or in working for her father. I did the best I could, but I can't say that I achieved the level of success I would have liked!

—Brooks Fenno, CMC, SALESMARK

they are in far more abundant supply than are "rainmaking skills." (If you don't believe that, just try to subcontract for delivery help and for business acquisition help. The former is so plentiful that the competition drives the fees down, the latter so rare as to be extremely difficult to acquire, and then at a considerable investment.)

Consequently, you must be willing and able to take business away from others. Most of us think that such rivalry occurs in the original sales process, but in fact it should occur even more frequently after buying decisions have been made. If you turn away from every prospect who is already using consultants, and if you believe that this is a "closed market" (a finite number of buyers) at all, then you're condemning yourself to a poor growth pattern because there are always going to be others who got there first.

But if you see anyone using consulting services as a legitimate prospect, then you're going to sharply increase your growth curve, since someone else getting there first can only improve your own chances. Burger King builds outlets across the street from McDonald's because they know that people are showing up there to buy hamburgers. Competition opens and expands markets; it doesn't narrow them.

When I hear that a firm has hired a rival, I don't say, "Drat, they beat me to it." I say, "Hmmm, how can I make the best of that?" Too many of us *take ourselves out of the running* by giving up far too early.

Here are a variety of techniques to use to trespass effectively on others' territory. Don't be pristine about this, because the best of them are trying to do it to you (so by turning these around, you also strengthen your own position within your clients). Some may appeal and some may not, so view them as a cafeteria of approaches.

Find a Different Buyer

Large organizations have a plethora of economic buyers, not always discernable by job title (a "director of knowledge management" may have budget and inclination to spend, while a "vice president of human resources" may have neither). Pursue a different division or department. Often, an intercompany rivalry will actually prompt a buyer to do something differently (hire you) for the same need from a "competitor" (who hired "them"). It's better to be a dueling consultant than not to have any part of the business at all.

Approach from a Different Direction

I've happily done executive retreats, keynote speeches, and even workshops in order to gain credibility and relationships in an organization where a competitor is doing what I really want to do, for example, strategy work or organizational redesign—one of the most effective assignments to "trespass" rapidly to executive coaching. This gains the trust and the ear of key decision makers. There are two keys in this "directional" technique:

1. You must have the diversity of consulting skills and related competencies (for example, speaking or facilitating) that allow for peripheral assignments.
2. You must "softly" but firmly reveal that you also work in the areas you're attacking, so that you're not typecast as a coach or facilitator who cannot do the real work you're targeting.

Parachute In

The overwhelming number of consultants form relationships at too low a level, and thereby constrain their own reach. For example, if a consultant can do workshops and strategy work but enters a company doing workshops, the executives will generally regard him or her as a trainer and a human resources specialist, and not credible at the strategic level. But if one enters at the latter level, it's relatively easy to go "down the ladder" to do workshops and retain executive credibility.

If the competition is at mid-levels—and particularly if they're confined to the HR department—make an unabashed pitch at executive levels. You won't even be considered competition with those already in place if you position yourself correctly. It's tough to prevent trespassers who ignore the huge fence and the danger signs and simply drop from the skies.

Leverage Through a Sponsor

I've spoken periodically of the power of trade associations, and the reason is that such groups really only have three functions: (1) lobby the government; (2) educate the public about the products or services of the industry; and (3) educate the members to perform better and to improve their businesses. It's this last category that is the toughest for them, and the one that we best address.

When a trade association sponsors you as a key resource, the members will tend to listen, no matter whom they are currently using. That's why speaking at major trade association events, with the implied or overt imprimatur of the association executives (and even if for free), is such a strong marketing technique and a good way to sneak in the back door behind your competition.

However, here's an even better method, which I've been using for some time: Take on the trade association itself as a client. This gives them real substance with which to endorse you, provides you with an invaluable reference and testimonial, and exposes you to the board and various committees composed of—you guessed it—high level member executives. If you do a great job here, you can unseat virtually any existing competition, no matter how entrenched or how large.

No one is so good or so entrenched that he or she can't be ousted. In fact, the longer a consulting firm is in place in a client, the more vulnerable it becomes unless it has taken steps to ensure its diversity of approach and multiplicity of buyers.

Belie the Fad

This one is only for the bold, but it's one of my favorites. This technique consists of burrowing in and blowing up the competition.

I will tell prospects that what they're doing is faddish and unproven. I never bad-mouth or speak negatively of the competition, but I will take strong and adverse positions on buzz words, academic nonsense, and stupid fads. In the course of this confrontation, I've taken on ridiculous stuff, including left brain/right brain thinking, fire walking, outdoor experiences, stewardship, servant leadership, reengineering, downsizing, TQM, shareholder value, future search, leaderless meetings, open book management, diversity training, and a raft of other stuff that I have truly believed belongs in comic books and not in corporate books.

Now, I don't ask that you agree with me on the examples, but I'm giving you a demonstration of how outspoken and forthright I tend to be. I tell prospects that these approaches are untested, ill-advised, sometimes unethical, and always more to the benefit of the seller than the buyer. I have facts and examples to back me up—this is not just one man's opinion. In those cases where the buyer needs a jolt of fresh air (and/or is mildly uncomfortable with what's been going on but has not chosen to stop the bandwagon), I make a quick inroad. In those cases when the buyer has a much different view from mine, well, nothing ventured, nothing gained. I didn't have the business anyway.

The One That Got Away

I recall many years ago making a "sales call" with a young consultant with whom I had rehearsed thoroughly on all the reasons this client should select us for this assignment—and do so now. Well, halfway through our presentation it was clear that we had this one in the bag. It was ours. And then what happened? My young consultant colleague simply couldn't resist. He had to make all the arguments we'd rehearsed. And then what do you supposed happened next?

Yep. The client began to get cold feet. Lots of second thoughts. Ever want to kill a colleague? The moral: It's okay to not shoot all your bullets!

—Bill Taylor, The Taylor Company

My last technique isn't for everyone, but it's been very effective for me. By showing the moxie it takes to confront a popular fad on the prospect's own turf, you also show the honesty and boldness that you'll provide as a consultant on assignment. For the buyers who honor that, fees are never important. And, fortunately or unfortunately, in twenty-six years in the business, the "woo woo" nonsense and the bizarre fads have remained embarrassingly in full view.

> If you don't have some favorite targets of approbation that you can easily and validly condemn with a prospect, then you just haven't been looking around very carefully. Take a stand. After all, you're pursuing business that someone else now owns. What can you lose?

FROM MY TIME IN THE TRENCHES

There is nothing wrong, unhealthy, unethical, immoral, or impure about trying to take a client from someone else so long as you believe you will provide more value and that you are respectful and honest toward the competition. Pursuing "low hanging fruit" is an ideal way to do this, since several of the normal resistance factors have already been overcome by someone else's hard work.

Stealing clients requires high visibility in general. But in the case of "waiting for someone else's bad news," you need targeted visibility, so that a "value campaign" can create an omnipresence. You can never be sure of being present at that exact time when the old relationship sours and the client needs someone new, but you can arrange to be within easy recall if you've bothered to provide demonstrable value and repute to your target. This can be managed with relatively few targets at any one time.

In some instances you want to create your own source of "bad news" by actively trespassing, which is not prohibited by law in consulting and seldom involves junk yard dogs or shotgun-wielding guards. You can breach fences, parachute in, or tunnel in. It can be a fine business practice, though a bold one, to take strong and adverse views about approaches (not people) that you believe to be, and can demonstrate to be, false, underperforming, or ephemeral.

Someone is trying to steal your clients. Use these techniques to form countermoves, but by all means consider others' clients as legitimate sources for your own marketing efforts.

CHAPTER 8

Guaranteeing the Ultimate Business: Repeat Business

How to Think of the Fourth Sale First

Early in my career one of my colleagues at an international training firm was a fellow named Mike Robert who became my co-author on the first book I (or he) ever published.[1] He was a very successful salesman and sales manager. When people asked him how to emulate his success, his stock answer was "think of the fourth sale first."

I've been running my own practice for seventeen years and, if you averaged my business origins over that time, you'd find that over 80 percent of my revenues are generated from previous clients, *and that over 90 percent of my business originates with buyers who have known me in one way or another.* In fact, I can trace the preponderance of my major accounts—single contracts of $50,000 and up—to less than a dozen sources.

---

1. *The Innovation Formula* (New York: HarperCollins, 1988).

That's right, like an anthropological exercise, the "roots" of my business come from just a relatively few sources. And that's even more dramatic when you consider that, in the early years of my practice, that network was far slimmer than it is today. To put it another way: That's a number in excess of $20 million generated by just a handful of people.

What does this mean for successful consultants? It means these four things:

1. Prior business is a gold mine that often isn't sufficiently exploited.
2. Prior buyers, not organizations, are the keys to future business acquisition.
3. The effort expended in business acquisition should decline as business acquisition grows.
4. Any truly new business from new sources should be treated as long-term business and not as a short-term project.

WHAT IS THE FOURTH SALE?

The "fourth sale" is a metaphor for thinking ahead. It means that grabbing business, completing it, and moving on, as if you're some kind of highway paving machine, doesn't create a very smooth road to future business with that client. If you set up the initial relationship as a partnership or collaboration that will form and reform itself as the buyer's conditions dictate, and not as a single interlude due to a unique issue, you are making many potential sales instead of one immediate sale.

Buyers think they are meeting with consultants for relief on a single issue. Consultants must recognize that such a meeting holds the potential for a permanent relationship that transcends business environments. What makes the difference for the direction of that relationship? You do.

Here is the genesis of a "fourth sale":

How to Acquire Clients

I receive quite a few inquiries which lead to business due to the fact that I successfully completed a major project with the Federal Reserve Bank of New York, the largest of the Federal Reserve banks and a very prestigious client.

The Federal Reserve buyers became clients on a reference from one of the banks it supervises and from an executive at that bank whom they trust. That buyer at that bank has been a client.

Prior to being a client at that bank, he was a client in running his own organization, where I assisted him with strategy and funding.

Prior to that, he was a buyer at another major bank in New York.

I met him at that original bank on a reference from someone I knew there after I had sent a letter and set of articles which, at the time (1985) cost 56 cents. We established a relationship, mutual trust, mutual respect, and reciprocity of interests that transcended any single environment. This was not a social friendship, but a business relationship.

Let me pause here. From that 56 cents and initial meeting, this individual has become responsible for over half a million dollars of business, including other organizations to which he has referred me. At the very origins of this particular "tree" is the person who recommended me to this buyer. He was an employee of the bank who went on to GE and provided me with business there. At that level, the resultant branches probably account for three-quarters of a million dollars. (I had met that person while working early in my career—with Mike Robert—at the training firm and had remained in touch and informed him when I had gone out on my own.)

I can provide a handful of examples like this one that have accounted for 90 percent of all my business. I must admit, I do not look back at these strands and interconnections and say, "Wow, was I fortunate!" Instead, I say, "Have I done everything I can to prolong and extend these connections?" Quite a few of them have petered out or reached dead ends. While this is inevitable, I constantly wonder if it were my fault in not sufficiently prompting, energizing, and nurturing these relationships.

In 1972 I conducted a training program that a human resources professional from Merck attended. We stayed in contact for eleven years while I worked in that account. In 1985, during the initial months of my solo practice, he tracked me down and suggested a project at Merck that I could bid on. Over the next twelve years his contacts and their contacts at Merck generated about 1.5 million dollars, and the interest in my work at Merck—for five years during that period "America's Most Admired Company" in the annual *Fortune* poll—resulted in millions of dollars in additional work. My original friend has since retired, although he once secured an assignment for me at another company from retirement through a friend who worked there. His effects on my career are with me every day.

> Ultimate consultants do not make sales or close on a project. They create and nurture trusting relationships which result in perpetual business connections.

Figure 8.1 shows the proper progression of effort to revenues. Irrespective of the economy, of your markets, of the competition, of technology, and of virtually all other external factors, you should be driving more revenues at less effort IF you have been "working on the fourth sale first." If you're a newer consultant, you must adapt and implement this philosophy immediately. If you're a successful veteran, you must ensure that you're exploiting these early contacts. If you're an unsuccessful veteran, you've been ignoring this relationship and working far harder than you should be.

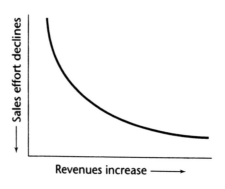

Figure 8.1. The Maturing Relationship Between Sales Effort and Revenues

How to Acquire Clients

THE THREE KEYS TO CEMENTING RELATIONSHIPS RATHER THAN SELLING BUSINESS

So how do we do this relentlessly and effectively? Most buyers are concerned about what's hurting them at the moment or about a singular opportunity that is making them salivate. They need results, not a friend. They're seeking relief, not more business for you.

My friend Mike Robert went on to establish his own international training and consulting firm. I decided to simply run my own practice and support the life style that was attractive to my family and me. I told Mike, with whom I've maintained a friendship, that he was always a better salesman than I was. "No," he said, "you're as good as I am, but while I sell programs and projects, you sell yourself. And no one can sell you the way that you do."

"Selling myself" really has meant establishing tight, trusting, and enduring relationships with people who can help me, and whom I can help, on a regular basis. As I've looked back and deconstructed the process, I believe the three secrets to this success are

1. Do not move rapidly toward a sale. Take the time to build a relationship first.
2. Do not content yourself with what the buyer wants. Search for the real need.
3. Do not consider the organization as your client. The buyer is your client, now and forever.

1. Do Not Move Rapidly Toward a Sale. Take the Time to Build a Relationship First. We do far too much work studying the organization, conducting needs analysis, and learning about the prospective company. We spend too little time understanding the buyer, raising emotional needs, and learning what would constitute personal success. If you truly believe that the goal is not a piece of business for next month but rather a flow of income for years, then answer these questions before you move on:

What will create trust between the buyer and me?
What emotional needs does the buyer express?
How can we work together, as a team?

Presentations and speeches at conferences or seminars are my most effective marketing technique. If you are knowledgeable about your subject and present well, your audience (potential clients) will naturally see your expertise, and then through conversation you will form the relationship. From that point on it is an easy sale.

Also, chairing a "CEO roundtable" at an appropriate group allows potential clients to get to know you over the course of a few months, see your style, gain trust in you, and then when they have a business challenge, you are a known quantity and foremost in their minds.

This, too, is an easy sale.

—Drumm McNaughton, The McNaughton Group, Inc.

Logic makes people think, emotion makes them act. A buyer may intellectually believe that you're good at what you do, and he or she may *react* to an inquiry positively because of that. But when a buyer *feels* that you're an invaluable asset, that person will *proactively* reach out to recommend you to others.

2. Do Not Content Yourself with What the Buyer Wants. Search for the Real Need. The buyer will tend to know immediately what he or she presumes is wanted. These are often commodities, such as sales training, coaching, communications skills, and so on. However, once a relationship is formed, some probing will generally turn up the real needs: improve retention of existing clients, end the turf warfare between departments, create a more positive growth curve, and so forth. Try to answer these questions before moving on:

Why is the buyer expressing this particular "want" or alternative?
What is the root cause of the symptoms being described?
How do we raise the standard and not merely fix the problem?

**3. *Do Not Consider the Organization as Your Client. The Buyer Is Your Client,
Now and Forever.*** This is the hardest for many consultants. "I work for Black &
Decker" is sexier than "I work for Harry Jones." But in truth, organizations don't
hire us, people do. And Black & Decker isn't going to refer you to more clients and
generate more business. Harry Jones is going to do that, if his needs have been
explored and met. Your objective is to find the right synergy in assisting both
Harry Jones and his organization. Try to answer these questions before moving on:

How can this project be implemented to reflect credit on the buyer?
How can I create an ongoing collaboration and dialogue with the buyer
despite having to work with subordinates on the implementation?
At what point can I begin to develop this relationship beyond the needs of
this particular project?

> Every single buyer knows what he or she wants before you walk in the
> door. Few of them truly understand what they need. The difference
> between what they think they want and what they truly need is your
> value added to that relationship and to that project. The project will
> end. The relationship shouldn't if you've provided enough value added.

Thinking of the fourth sale first is counterintuitive. It means resisting the
immediate sale and subordinating the organizational environment for the
moment. The key is to focus on the buyer as someone with whom you want to
develop a long-term relationship. It's like focusing on your swing in golf and not
on hitting the ball. You have to exercise patience and restraint. This is a philosophy
and a value system. The techniques themselves are not difficult, but the volition is.

A referral is a very quick means to get business. Ironically, it results from a
slow and steady gait at the outset, which might have been years prior.

DEVELOPING TRUST THROUGH PUSHBACK

The critical path to trust and long-term relationships is not in agreement and
harmony. It is in disagreement and creative tension.

I call this tactic "pushback," by which I mean the healthy resistance to a buyer's position. Buyers are surrounded by "yes people," whose future, retirement plans, and stress levels are often dictated by their own perceptions of the need to please their boss. The higher you ascend in an organization, the truer this is. While a first-line supervisor has a very real grasp of the world, since he or she is also dealing with customers all day long, a middle manager has a somewhat distorted view, half-shaded by subordinates' versions of reality. By the time you reach the executive suites, there is often a complete disconnect, with committees, reports, task forces, and other information avenues so jaded and filtered that the vice presidents are like the general staff in 18th Century England, waiting for carrier pigeons to bring delayed news of the battles on the Continent. By the time the birds land, conditions have already changed.

Buyers don't need more sycophants or obsequiousness. They need candor. Challenging a buyer's position and beliefs also serves as a strong "fourth sale litmus test": If the buyer doesn't respond well to your pushback, the chances of a longer term relationship are remote. In that case, you may choose to take the money and run, or simply run.

Here are some areas in which to consider pushback, and techniques to employ in so doing.

Basic Premises

This one is my favorite. The buyer is often likely to travel far and wide on a set of beliefs that have no validation to support them. When a buyer says, "People are less loyal today, so we need an incentive system that is leveraged toward the longer term to force them to stay," I'll typically respond, "I disagree with your basic premise. There are no studies supporting the position that employees are any less loyal inherently, but there are studies that show that organizations have forfeited that loyalty. Perhaps we can re-establish it here without increasing the incentive system at all."

You'll often find that a buyer has spent a long time thinking about an issue and has strong views on cause and effect, but the amount of time spent pondering it does not equal a quality conclusion. In other words, a lot of time thinking about the wrong factors leads you nowhere.

Listen carefully to your buyer's foundations for his or her argument. Push back on any that are questionable, unproved, weak, or vulnerable. Help the buyer to see, from the outset, that his or her best interests are going to be served by your role in helping to validate or invalidate basic beliefs about the situation. The probability is very strong that no one else is attempting that role.

Pushback is the technique of demonstrating to the buyer that his or her best interests are served by a partner who is respectful and honest enough to disagree, thereby helping to avoid potential disaster later on.

Immediate Options

Buyers, particularly highly assertive buyers, will have their pet and favored treatments, solutions, and courses of action all dressed up and ready to parade. The problem, of course, is that they are prematurely limiting their own success.

My preference is to explain to any buyer that there are always plenty of options and rarely only one solution. The key is the "risk/reward ratio." In other words, how much reward at how much risk? No plan or project is risk-free. But we can work together to mitigate the risks if we understand them in relation to the potential rewards. Rolling out a pilot is lower risk, but the ultimate impact is also far less than a full-scale launch. Hiring people quickly to fill vacancies provides a quick fix, but the risk of lower quality and mistakes with key accounts must be weighed.

Figure 8.2 shows an example of a formalized risk/reward template that can focus a buyer on his or her best interests and on how the two of you can work together to exploit the rewards while mitigating the risks.

The True Change Agent

I've been told bluntly, "Well, you're the change agent. What will you do to help us fix this?" To which I've replied, "You're the change agent, not me. We'd better clarify who's doing what to whom."

Many clients don't know how to use consultants, even though they may have hired them before (which is why re-education is always constructive and helpful for both of you). Organizational improvement is the client's responsibility, and the buyer will be evaluated for the results. The consultant

Selling is not just about new business; it's about influencing others through their emotional "triggers."

I "sold" Kaiser Permanente on authorizing payment for a machine my daughter Margo needed for her cystic fibrosis. I went in with lots of proof statements to a group of analysts, accountants, actuaries, and customer service managers. I realized they were all mothers and started talking about four-year-olds and how tough they were to figure out and understand.

The mothers warmed up to me, and the meeting went well. By personalizing the issue, I won them over and stood out from many other parents who come into those meetings with both guns blazing.

—Andrew J. Birol, PACER Associates, Inc.

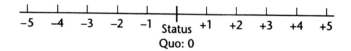

Question: What is the best and worst that might result?

+5 = Paradigm-breaking improvement, industry leader
+4 = Dramatic improvement, major publicity
+3 = Strong benefits, organization-wide
+2 = Minor benefits, localized
+1 = Very minor improvement, barely noticed

−1 = Very minor setback, barely noticed
−2 = Minor setback, controlled locally
−3 = Public setback, requires damage control
−4 = Major defeat, financial damages, recovery time needed
−5 = Devastating losses

Figure 8.2. The Risk/Reward Ratio

is a resource and catalyst, perhaps, but is, by definition, someone without authority.

If I can successfully reorient a buyer to understand a better paradigm for our potential work together, the resultant fee is not going to be an issue. It will also create the criteria for an excellent, long-term relationship based on the correct rules of engagement: Consultants advise; managers act.

> Relationships are based on trust; trust is based on mutual respect; respect is based on both parties' ability and willingness to constructively disagree, with the intent of creating a better future. Ask managers which subordinates they *respect* the most, and it won't be their best friends or the "yes people." It will be those who consistently support a clear value system.

Here are some excellent "pushback" lines that can quickly test whether the buyer is looking for a peer and partner, or simply wants "another pair of hands and no disagreements":

"We can't go any further exploring this project until we gain resolution on these key issues."

"In my experience, I can't let you do this without explaining the risks. If we can't have that discussion, we probably shouldn't proceed."

"Those objectives are in direct conflict, and one of them is going to have to go."

"What is that assumption based on? Who told you? Have you validated it with your customers or employees?"

"You're describing symptoms and effects. We should examine the causes if we're really going to resolve the issue."

"Why fix this at all? Shouldn't we be trying to raise the standard rather than conform to the old one?"

"Isn't that goal arbitrary? Why settle for 10 percent? Why not try to maximize the growth? Maybe 25 percent is actually achievable if we don't limit expectations."

"If you stopped doing this altogether, would the customer notice at all? If you implement this new initiative, would the customer notice at all?"

"What criteria did you use to set the priority here? Are we sure it's not simply a matter of the 'squeakiest wheel' instead of the most pressing business need?"

"Let me play devil's advocate. . . ."

Who Could Make This Up?

I was introduced to the CEO of State Street Bank, who was told I was being considered as the consultant to assist with an organization-wide initiative. He was in a huge, well-appointed office and commanded one of the most profitable financial institutions around, with an excellent personal track record.

"We've had an average of 22 percent annual compound growth annually for my entire watch, five years," he said calmly. "Why would we need a consultant?"

I thought for a few seconds, then looked him in the eye and said, "How do you know it shouldn't be 34 percent?"

I got the job.

—AW

THE PRESENT-VALUE DISCOUNT PRINCIPLE IN ACTION

I needed a fancy title to gain your attention for a simple concept: Loyalty formed by trust is hard to displace. In fact, you can view this section as the antidote to Chapter 7, on the assumption that there are people out there employing some sophisticated techniques to try to capture your best customers at your expense.

> You can't hang on to any client forever. But you can extend most relationships through multiple engagements. This is why specialization is anathema to ensuring long-term, high quality repeat business from any one client.

Your buyer is going to be exposed to your competition. There will be some organizational resistance to your continued participation, emanating from those whom you've threatened (often by your mere presence). Budgets will change.

Nevertheless, the buyer literally can't "buy" the type of relationship the two of you have formed over the course of your projects together. This can't be instantly replaced, and that trust, reliance, and sometimes dependence is not immediately transferable. Consequently, even a competitor offering a substantially lower fee isn't going to be a sound return on investment because the value proposition will perforce be less, since that competitor can't match your history with the buyer.

Therefore, that history must be carefully created and maintained. If you believe for a moment that repeat business—relatively unaffected by fees—is dependent on your relationship with your buyer, then you can agree that the relationship requires as much strategy and forethought as does the project. (If you don't agree with that, then you're reading the wrong book and the wrong author.) The problem that undermines enduring repeat business, then, is that the relationship is ignored in favor of the project, since the consultant *incorrectly* assumes that a completed, successful project is all that's needed to support the relationship (or, worse, is not even thinking in terms of the fourth sale).

I can make a strong case that, if you're interested in improving business acquisition with a minimum of cost, then your existing clients are your major source. And if they are your major source, then these are the steps that you can't afford to ignore. *Most consultants have up and down years, impossible forecasting scenarios, and a lot of work to bring in revenue, because they don't gain sufficient renewal business.* If you take nothing else from this book, consider the following tactics.

Ten Steps to Ensure Long-Term, High-Fee Renewal Business

1. *Never sacrifice or abandon the buyer.* No matter to whom you are delegated, referred, or aligned, assertively make plans with your buyer for periodic personal interaction. Don't pat yourself on the back after the contract is signed and relax with lower level implementers. If you're not seeing the buyer in person at least twice a month, then you're not developing the trust and loyalty you'll need.

2. *Bring the buyer good news.* Many consultants bring the buyer their problems. Problems are much better digested when they are a small ration of good news that's more frequent. Share successes and small victories. Inform the buyer of your progress constructively.

3. *Assign the buyer accountabilities.* My proposals all have a section specifying "joint accountabilities." Ensure that the buyer is a partner and an integral part of the project. Otherwise, you're just another hired hand reporting to the buyer.

4. *Suggest and recommend actions in non-project areas.* I once spotted clear examples of a hostile work environment while working on an unrelated issue. I informed the buyer and emphasized his exposure, then offered to work with human resources on a resolution "while I was on-site anyway." If you ought to provide value prior to securing a sale, you should also provide value *prior to securing repeat sales.*

Scope creep occurs when a buyer asks you for help outside of the objectives of your project. But value contribution occurs when you volunteer help in view of your observations and experience. The former should be avoided, but the latter should be maximized.

---

5. *Demonstrate that you have wide-ranging capabilities.* Talk about other projects, other clients, other methodologies. Don't be stereotyped as a facilitator, strategist, or coach if you can possibly help it. Assuming you've developed the skills by this stage of your career to be diverse, expose those skills to the buyer. *Specialists have a very tough time gaining renewal business because the narrower the specialty, the less likely there are more opportunities to apply it within a single client.*

6. *Be flexible.* The client might need you for a weekend, or want to talk on a Sunday night, or ask that you work with an employee whom you consider to be a lost cause. Show the client that you can be counted on, especially when the deadlines are short or conditions abruptly change. Occasionally, you might have to miss an airplane in order to catch more business. There are other airplanes.

7. *Reach out laterally to more buyers.* This not only protects you in the event your buyer leaves, but it creates a "mass loyalty," which is even harder for competition to overcome. I've been in organizations in which all departments had to go through my strategy approach, or attend my communications workshop, or have the division head coached by me. It became a rite of passage. This is the exact and positive opposite of the organizational "immune system" rejecting you.

8. *Implement approaches using your proprietary materials, copyright, intellectual property, buzz words, and so on.* Make the projects "uniquely" you. The more generic your approach, the more others can smoothly move in to replace you. The more customized and client-specific your approach, the more you become irreplaceable. Develop some joint copyrights with the client and become enmeshed in the systemic processes you work with.

9. *The time to "sell" your next project is while you're still there on the current project.* As you advise and observe, listen for buying signs such as, "We really do need to look into that." Offer to submit a proposal so that the buyer will have something to utilize "whenever you're ready to move on this." Don't assume that you must complete the current project before pristinely bidding on a new one. That's why constant meetings and reporting are much more important and effective than waiting until a magic "completion" date.

There is nothing unethical or immoral about pursuing additional projects while working on a current one if you take the position that you are able to improve your client's condition in so doing. In fact, there are no doubt economies of scale that imbue to your working on several projects at once. This isn't about *resources;* it's about *trust.*

The One That Got Away

The "king" who appears to be the decision maker and may, in fact, be the decision maker, can be rendered useless if the "dukes" don't go along after the sale.

I once sold a $300,000 project to a large bank. The vice chairman of the company and a couple of his colleagues in the office of the chairman decided that the project I'd proposed was the right project. They gave agreement, signed the deal, and communicated it to their people.

About three weeks into the project, several of their regional managers decided that the project was too threatening to them and, to make a long story short, brought the project to a halt and had us fired. It was over within twenty-four hours. They had "nodded" their agreement to the vice chairman before the engagement started and pulled out their knives after he turned his head. He said, "I'm really sorry to have to tell you this, but it's over."

The lessons were: (1) It ain't really sold until the people who have to change or implement the solution are sold and (2) Never do work that the client should be doing in terms of aligning people internally and holding them accountable. If the "big guy" is really committed to the result, and you've sold the path to the result, you can lay out the path, but you can't MAKE them walk down it.

—Nick Miller, Clarity Advantage Corporation

10. *If you are between projects, stay in touch.* "Well, you know how to reach me if you need me" is probably a candidate for the Marketing Hall of Shame. Out of sight, out of mind. Your successful project's "glow" will have an alarmingly brief life span. Try to continue to talk to the buyer monthly on any constructive pretext: follow-up, new ideas, breakfast or lunch, news from your other clients, objective sounding board—anything it takes to keep you in front of your decision maker and to maintain the trust that you've built.

Thinking of the fourth sale first is a philosophy that must be applied to every lead that comes down the pike. There will be clients with whom a single project makes sense. There will be others who produce conditions making repeat business improbable or impossible.

However, the crime occurs when the consultant is the party responsible for no fourth sale (or even a second sale!). If, from early in one's career, the effort had been made to aggressively turn every single new client into a long-term customer, any reader of this book would have generated well into six figures or more of additional income. If you're new to the game, don't make this mistake. If you're a veteran, mine the rich lode that you've already created by blasting your way into the place to begin with.

FROM MY TIME IN THE TRENCHES

Our long-term success thrives on renewal business. This occurs in two primary ways:

1. Additional business from client organizations.
2. Additional business from prior buyers who have moved to new organizations.

Thinking of the "fourth sale first" simply means viewing any prospect with the intent of creating an enduring relationship and not a quick sale. In fact, forsaking the quick sale and using the patience required to build a relationship can be a far more productive business strategy for virtually anyone.

Relationships are based on trust, which in turn is based on candor. We have to "push back" if buyers are to view us as credible peers and not as subordinates, hired hands, or contractors. Healthy and constructive challenges early in the relationship building process will serve both to weed out non-attractive buyers and to solidify the trust of mature and confident buyers.

Note that none of this is based on or involves fees. In fact, fees become academic when strong relationships exist.

> It's one thing to lose business to the competition, but it's another entirely to give it away. With apologies to Dylan Thomas, don't go gently into that good night.

It is extremely difficult and often impossible for a competitor to replace an incumbent consultant who has developed a legacy of trust and reliance. By instituting certain techniques, such as proprietary materials and value-added additional recommendations, it's feasible to create a "norm" of using your help in every department of the client company.

Think in terms of acquiring *business*, not necessarily *clients*. That's because you already have the clients, so why make life more difficult?

CHAPTER 9

A Dozen New Sources of Clients

*The World Is Changing and
So Are Your Prospects*

As I write this, my prior fiscal year was my finest ever. Yet it was a year prior to which I had decided to cut back, further decrease my travel, and accept lower revenues at a time in my career when I could clearly afford to do so.

Shows what I know.

The fact is, during my "ascendant" years, when my brand as "the million dollar consultant" began to take shape, I was deriving 75 percent of my income from traditional consulting with traditional firms: Merck, Marine Midland Bank, Times Mirror, Calgon, Mercedes-Benz, and others like them. The other 25 percent derived from workshops with firms such as GE, GTE, IBM, Fleet Bank, Texaco, the *New York Times*, and their counterparts. I thought that was my world. I occasionally worked overseas at the direction of U.S.-based multinationals.

Today, more successful than ever, about 25 percent of my

income originates with traditional consulting with traditional firms. About 40 percent is generated by innovative consulting assignments: Consulting with other consulting firms, such as Andersen, Cambridge-Pharma, and Peat Marwick; consulting with major high-tech organizations, such as Hewlett-Packard; and consulting with entrepreneurial start-ups, such as Burst! Multimedia, an Internet advertising operation.[1] And about 35 percent—a full third of my practice—comes from sources that did not exist for me ten years ago: product sales, mentoring, coaching, publishing, and joint ventures. And, for the first time, I'm being hired by foreign-based organizations without a major U.S. presence, such as Solving, International.

I'm constantly surprised by how stupid I was two weeks ago.

I've been open to change and experimentation. Success, which most of the readers of this book enjoy, enables you to take prudent risk and explore new territory. Ironically, in searching for ways to increase my comfort and decrease the unattractive aspects of the profession (travel, unpleasant clients, economic fluctuation), I've stumbled on even more profitable methods to sustain my business. This has often been wonderful serendipity, but the harder I work the luckier I get.

Some sources of revenue are eternal; some are ephemeral, and disappear. But what about those which are just beginning to demonstrate their potential? Do you know what and where they are?

But what would happen if we tried to predict the most lucrative potential business acquisition sources waiting around the bend? I'm no futurist (who really is?) and don't claim to be a prognosticator. But my track record is better than most, so herein—my gift to you—are my suggestions for areas you should plumb now to derive new and important sources of business over the next decade. If they're well-known to you and you're already well-established, then you may proceed to Chapter 10 with my blessing.

---

1. As an example that buyer loyalty is more important than "corporate" loyalty, Burst! originated with a former buyer at *Business Week* and the Times Mirror Corp.

1. GLOBAL ALLIANCES

We are often besieged with "offers to collaborate" from unknown parties in strange places who would like to see all of our materials and proprietary approaches as a condition of being considered for their "amazing opportunity" in Upper Bizarristan! I'm not talking about these con artists. I am referring to a particularly happy confluence of events that makes us valuable overseas.

American management expertise is highly regarded—probably more so than ever before. Most of the world is speaking English (to the abject horror of the French) and the U.S. dollar is so powerful and omnipresent that most of the currency is actually in circulation outside of the U.S. and several countries have officially adopted it as their standard.

Established American consultants should examine reaching out to consulting firms in major international locations that can use their marketing, delivery, and technological expertise in high potential local markets. These alliances can take the form of consulting to the consulting firm and/or participating as a resource in their own acquisition and delivery of business.

While this opportunity exists to some extent in the reverse—non-U.S. consultants offering help here—it is basically an export phenomenon and may grow prodigiously.

Action: Extend your brand internationally, consider publishing and/or appearing as a speaker internationally, and locate those firms that can profit from your expertise and approaches.

Example: I was recently asked to keynote an important Asia/Pacific conference based on my publishing and repute. I immediately began to establish contacts in Australia and New Zealand to explore the potential of a joint venture during my visit.

2. REMOTE LEARNING

The nascent attempts to create online learning have been laughably inept. The content, presentation, speed of download, lack of interaction, and other factors have undermined the effort. However, the thirst for lifelong, remote learning that drives such attempts is real and growing. One of the innovators in this area, the University of Phoenix, has been growing dramatically.

Many of my colleagues have begun coaching exclusively by phone and email. My own mentor program is predominantly conducted by phone, email, and fax. What aspects of your current (or easily developed) technology and methodology can be adapted for distance learning?

My belief is that "real time" consulting will be more urgent than ever: The executive who is facing a sudden crisis, the sales manager staring at a key contract, the call center director encountering a technology glitch. This is highly valuable assistance, because it is aimed at crucial opportunities, problems, and issues the value of which is immediately apparent. Yet the odds of the consultant, even on retainer, being present when they occur are very long.

Urgency and immediate need can short-cut the relationship building process, especially for veteran consultants with a strong brand. Moreover, you don't need conceptual agreement when the client's office is on fire.

Are there ways you can make yourself and your help available—whether to existing clients or to non-clients who can readily find you—on a "real time" basis? Why can't you launch a service that doesn't require that you be on an airplane but does pay well because of the clear value added?

Action: Examine what you do for its applicability on a distance basis. Reconfigure it to maximize distance user–friendliness.

Example: Why not a twenty-four-hour "on call" responsiveness using pager technology for a fee of $50,000 a month, but assisting the client in averting calamity and exploiting fast-breaking opportunity? Is a guarantee to call back within an hour at that rate of pay better or worse than logging 200,000 air miles annually for small projects?

Use the fifteen-minute rule. That is, leaving if you are kept waiting longer than that when meeting with a prospect. The upside is great (if they call you back, your meeting will be much better), but the downside is the most important. If they were not really serious, you got away without "spilling your candy in the lobby."

—Andrew J. Birol, PACER Associates, Inc.

3. ENTREPRENEURS

The downsizing of the Eighties and Nineties, coupled with the technological apogee and perigee of the late Nineties through current times, have created a new brand of entrepreneurs. These are people who refuse to place their fates in others' hands, will not risk someone else firing them, and who truly believe in taking prudent risk in return for dramatic reward. (Sound familiar?)

A decade ago, venture capital was used solely for research and development (Let's get ahead of the competition) and marketing (Let's tell people what we've got). Today, venture capital is also allocated to management support, in that the hard lessons of high turnover, poor selection decisions, lack of training, and related human resource issues have been understood. Brilliant technology and a receptive market won't overcome poor sales, lousy customer service, and low productivity.

There is a market segment for consultants consisting of these entrepreneurs, who are not as narrow and specialized as their prototypes. They have often built decent-sized operations and realize that the founders and builders are not the people to run them (or to run them unassisted). The entrepreneur has matured and constitutes a business segment for consultants no less than corporate executives or trade associations.

Action: You are an entrepreneur and should instantly relate to such buyers. Join groups and network with these prospects. Reorient your value proposition to appeal to the strong-willed, successful, self-made person.

Example: Many universities and business groups (such as The Executive Technique, The Business Roundtable) conduct formalized programs to embrace entrepreneurs. You should be referenced as a business resource, just as a highly respected internist or attorney is referenced for his or her particular professional expertise. A $100,000 fee from an entrepreneur carries the same purchasing power as a $100,000 fee from General Motors, but comes with fewer strings and less filtering.

Entrepreneurs don't care about your small size, your background, or your having been fired earlier in life. They care about what you can do for them and their prized business tomorrow. You can do a lot, because you've created that same kind of business.

---

4. UNIVERSITIES AND HIGHER EDUCATION

Universities have had a problem for quite some time with excess delivery capability. They have tenured professors, classrooms, research, and other resources that aren't fully employed and are increasing under competitive pressure from new sources (remote learning, corporate "universities," and so on). They have countered with extension programs, consulting offerings, teleconferencing, and other devices to wedge themselves into the general market. Case Western Reserve University is just one example of a very aggressive entity in this area, offering a comprehensive range of management training for member companies.

The problem, of course, is that the intellectual and delivery resources that most universities solely "own" are, well, professors. And they are not exactly attuned to the real world, pragmatic, and rapidly changing needs of modern corporate life. (Academics: Please send your letters to Jossey-Bass/Pfeiffer, not to me.) Let's face it, if you lose a deal to a moonlighting college professor you're in the wrong line of work, even if the professor offers to do it for free.

Reach out to local universities first, offering both to consult with them on their business development plans and to serve as a resource that they can uniquely bring to their intended prospects. One seasoned consultant can offset a lot of academic pie in the sky. And you can let your partner do all the marketing.

Action: Select the local institutions of higher learning most likely to be amenable, and find the dean or director responsible for executive and corporate outreach. You might also want to pursue those schools nationally that already have a reputation for doing this well.

Example: Case Western Reserve markets the programs, pays the consultant to address its groups, and then allows the consultant to pursue and own whatever business may ensue from those contacts.

5. THE PROFESSIONS: MEDICAL, LEGAL, ACCOUNTING

Whatever I'm about to suggest here can also be applied to realtors, architects, and others. But I want to focus on the "major" professions curiously allied to our own.

I'm increasingly being asked by legal firms to address them and work with them on the issues of value-based fees and business acquisition. I've helped a colleague to specialize in the valuation, sale, and transfer of medical practices. Accounting firms that have not gone into consulting themselves are increasingly squeezed by their hourly, primitive billing practices.

These are professions, in my view, that are just beginning to creep out from under their own specialist tarps. They are seeing the light of increased business and the need for marketing and more intelligent pricing. Their past people policies (make partner or leave) would have been envied by Captain Bligh. All of that is changing because of younger partners taking over, changing business conditions, and competitive pressures.

> Specialized professional practices know as little about everything else as they know a great deal about their specialty. You can't teach a law firm the law, but you can teach them virtually everything else about how to run a business.

I don't think it requires much to "slide" your promotion and marketing into these areas. They are virtually untouched, and the last thing they need is still more legal, medical, and financial advice.

Action: Embrace these professions in your collateral materials and website. Speak at their trade associations. Ask your own doctor, dentist, lawyer, and accountant to sponsor or recommend you.

Example: There are law firms with over five hundred attorneys, medical practices that are incorporated and embrace many specialties, and accountancies that are multi-national. These are no different from major corporate accounts except for their content.

6. MATURE HIGH-TECH

We're entering the wonderful world of "post-shakeout." The high-tech firms that remain have been sufficiently aged, matured, and weathered. They now need to stabilize and run themselves well. (Even Amazon.com will eventually run out of growth room and will have to demonstrate a profit.)

You needn't be a technology expert—in fact, you shouldn't be—to provide the kind of stabilization and managed growth advice that these firms desperately need. This is why I've always stressed "process consulting," in that the content isn't very important in terms of the correct management decisions and orientation.

This, too, is a virtually untapped area, although there is so much precedent. Hewlett-Packard has long been a leading user of consultants, and it represents an early version of a matured high-tech company. Motorola, Texas

Instruments, and, of course, IBM are no different. The Apples and Dells are perhaps in their young adulthood, beginning to truly appreciate the value of external help. There are, however, a plethora of adolescent firms that are fodder right now for enterprising consultants.

It's time to stop treating "high-tech" as a specialty area for programmers, coders, and Internet wizards. View them as an increased part of your market.

Action: These firms are all over the place. Begin to prospect for the mid-sized to larger firm that has survived the turmoil and is rife for professional help. In these firms the economic buyer is almost always at the CEO level and nowhere below that.

Example: Many of these firms are run by people who are refugees from the "old economy" and aren't "technocrats" at all. They are probably the best prospects because they'll appreciate the value of sound management practices.

> There are going to be more people who are affluent, educated, officially retired, and in search of meaning and fulfillment than ever before in our history. That demographic cries out for you to find a way to address it.

7. THE RETIRED, THE RECREATING, THE HOBBYIST

We have a more affluent, more educated, younger retired cohort in our population than ever before. Geriatric medicine, overlooked as a backwater specialty twenty years or so ago, is now an important branch of the science. There are leisure cruises, elder care, assisted living, and other nice marketing initiatives aimed at the demographic of fifty-five and older. The American Association of Retired People is the best funded, most powerful lobby in America.

And now the Baby Boomers are entering that age bracket, which will swell like a flood-stage river enveloping the surrounding plains.

The Twilight Zone

The most unusual situation I've encountered was where I was set up with the economic buyer by an internal qualifier. Five minutes into my presentation, the buyer said, "Stop. You're hired. That example of work you just showed me is exactly the expertise I'm looking for." (That situation took me to the Netherlands and my first real international consulting/training gig.)

Another example: I was hired as a subcontractor by a company that was also a subcontractor to the firm that was ultimately hired by the actual buyer. I went into the first engagement stone cold without knowing anything about the buyer or their situation, and in less than two hours I had their legal department rewriting their client contracts and had expanded their prospect approach from one service to four services. You never know until you ask!

—David Hamacher, President, Communicon Consulting Group, Inc.

While the individual market may not be your priority (though for some of you it may be or should be), these people belong to increasingly large and powerful organizations. What were once minor hobbyist and recreation groups now have tens of thousands of members and require administration, promotion, governance, staff development, and a myriad of other organizational consulting needs. Budgets are often in the millions of dollars, and the competition for this group—which is benefiting from the IRA legislation of the Eighties and does not have to save money for home, children, or retirement—is intense among interests ranging from sports equipment and vacations to dietary care and volunteer work.

It is also a group seeking continued lifelong learning, meaning that individual product sales for self-fulfillment, second careers, special causes, and so on can be highly lucrative.

Action: Consider shifting your focus or additionally embracing the associations, groups, and causes that the growing age fifty-five plus population focuses on. This demographic has more discretionary buying power than any other group, including teenagers.

Example: Groups such as the American Philatelic Society, which appeal mainly to an older populace, must consider expanding offerings, moving to new locations, creating new member services, educating board members responsible for large budgets, and so forth. This is process consulting simply refocused on a different potential client.

> The Baby Boomer influence will be felt through the entire first quarter or more of the 21st Century, as a new, powerful, and wealthy retired population continues to grow and to make demands on the society, economy, and technology.

8. BEHAVIOR MODIFICATION

My projection is that the pop psychology approaches of the Nineties, from walking on hot coals to rappelling down mountains, will give way to a more pragmatic and widespread interest in legitimate and long-term behavioral change. Just as massive public education efforts dramatically reduced smoking in most countries, there will be increasing practical and valid approaches needed for weight control, civility (for example, countering road rage), personal relationships (decreasing the current high divorce rates), raising children in a complex time, substance abuse control, improving career choices, and so on.

These are areas that will primarily be pursued on an individual level, meaning that interactions such as workshops, corporate sponsorships, seminars, products, coaching, Internet access, and other individualized techniques will be highly appropriate. Unlike today's "feel good for the moment" environment, in which a motivational speech's sweetness also has a sugar donut's nutritional value, the need will be for legitimate, credentialed sources to provide help in truly affecting individual habits, traits, and behaviors.

Action: Examine the degree to which your organizational change work is really based on individual change and how that can be marketed and delivered to that new audience. Alliances and sponsorships may be very effective for these purposes.

Example: You may develop a booklet or manual on controlling hostility which is distributed for you through an association to its membership. Or you may provide web-based coaching on how to control anger to individuals who either pay for it themselves or are reimbursed by their organizations.

9. LIFE BALANCE

I began a life balance newsletter[2] called *Balancing Act: Blending Life, Work, and Relationships* with forty names in 1999. Today, it has over five thousand subscribers. Although the newsletter is free, its presence generates tremendous word-of-mouth promotion for my consulting, speaking, and product sales.

Most of our consulting expertise is applicable to individual and social circumstances, from building relationships and influencing others to solving problems and setting priorities. Once we blur the work/personal line, we're able to deal holistically with people's total lives, making all aspects of them that much more productive and rewarding.

Corporations such as Hewlett-Packard and Levi Strauss have been in the forefront of helping employees in all aspects of their work and lives, and others will continue to follow suit as a relatively inexpensive alternative to building loyalty and enhancing performance. My belief is that a consultant who can both advise an organization on its needs *and* advise its employees on their needs is an extraordinary asset, able to transcend those environments.

Action: Include in your offerings to clients options to provide non-work-related assistance during the course of your projects. You may choose to do this yourself if you have the competencies, or subcontract such work.

Example: If your expertise is organizational change, why not offer workshops to employees and their partners on how to plan for and react to personal change? If you deal with finance for non-financial managers, why not offer an analogous process for budgeting and investment as an option for employees?

---

2. It's free and if you'd like to subscribe simply send an email to join-balancingact@summitconsulting.com.

> Life balance issues are not a fad and are growing. Yet the corporation may be the entity that pays for their resolution. This may be a shift you can make immediately in current clients, as well as an option you include for all future clients.

10. SALES SKILLS

This is a perennial need if there ever was one. In more than twenty-seven years of consulting, the need to influence a buyer has been uninterrupted, as it has been since subsistence farming ended and the first farmer with more than his own family could eat was persuaded to part with excess crops in return for a new tool or tutoring for a child.

Among the areas most in need of sales skills in the next decade:

Telemarketing
Relationship and consultative sales
Professional practice sales (medical, law, financial, real estate, architecture)
Global sales that are cross-cultural
Value-based sales (as opposed to commodities)
Luxuries rather than necessities
Services more than products
Fund raising and grants

Action: If you're in the sales skills arena, broaden those processes you currently use to include other areas. They are much more similar than dissimilar. If you're not in that market, consider your existing process strengths and how they relate to sales, for example, negotiating, conflict resolution, communications, and so forth.

Example: Call centers are big business, and growing. Why can't "order takers" and service representatives become skilled in "upselling" and providing additional products and services? The investment is already made, and further sales are largely profit.

The One That Got Away

This was a lead in one of the largest providers of credit cards in the United States, which recently had been charged by the federal government with interest rate and consumer fraud. They called seeking a customer satisfaction program in a hurry. We were to be part of a "Pillsbury Bake-Off®" with three other firms, two of which were industry powerhouses and one a local firm with no brand recognition. During the presentation, we "sold in" to the senior VP and the president as the decision makers. There were a couple of mid-level manager/coordinators in the room, one of whom was taking copious notes and not saying much (nor did we ask much). After several days of nail biting, what ifs, and dwindling hopes, my partner heard from the project manager. We did not get the business. Here are the morals of the story.

1. Never, ever, accept title as a given for who will be the final decision maker. Never dismiss lower level titles. Sell in to every person at the table, with the value-added information that works for them. This requires questioning, listening, and responding to each person's concerns.

The project manager was not in fact the client contact at all (and was also blindsided in the process). The mid-level supervisor who was furiously writing notes as we confidently sold in to "the big boys" was actually given responsibility for the project. The VP left it up to her to decide which firm to use, and although he "didn't agree with her," felt he "had to support her." We clearly had not addressed her concerns, and since this was to be a custom designed project, client coordination would be extremely important. Being an inexperienced project manager, the extent of coordination made her very apprehensive.

2. Don't make assumptions as to the viability of the competition, and

3. Don't assume that the prospect always wants, or cares about, your ideal world solution. The two industry powerhouses lost out as well. A very small local firm, proposing the use of canned videos, won the contract. They offered a quick and easy fix with less stress for the mid-level project manager. It turns out that the bank really didn't care about customer satisfaction and developing a comprehensive solution. A contract to wave in front of the judge to show compliance fit the bill nicely.

—Barbara Poole, President, Poole Resources, Inc.

11. CULTURAL ACCOMMODATION

Our society is changing dramatically. In 2001, more women than men entered law school, which will have a profound influence on power and politics in ten to twenty years. The Hispanic population is the fastest growing minority. This will influence buying trends and employment. Disabled and physically challenged people continue to enter the labor pool and hold responsible positions, thanks to both changing attitudes and appropriate legislation.

The customer base and the employee base should mirror each other. And the advent of global sales for even small operations further complicates the process. The "diversity industry" of the late Nineties has proven itself to be after a dollar more than after organizational change. (How can anyone be a "diversity consultant" who is not an organizational development consultant?) The future isn't about pretending to honor "differences." It is about the pragmatic fact that studies have supported the power and productivity of heterogeneous work teams over homogeneous work teams.[3]

Consultants can help organizations that still have leaders who grew up in simpler times and different demographic realities. This will be a key productivity enhancement area.

Action: Incorporate not just the "people side" into your change initiatives, but the diverse people side that modern organizations must accommodate if they are to be competitive and effective.

Example: Build your global experiences and your credential in dealing with diverse work forces and customer bases. Pursue international work as both a welcome aspect of a successful practice and an important component of your ability to stay current.

---

3. Which is why the United States is much more productive and innovative than Japan, mythology notwithstanding.

> The cultural differences that exist among organizational units are analogous to those which exist among people of differing backgrounds. Experiences, values, nurturing, friends, assimilation, and other factors are at work. They need to be addressed by consultants, not by diversity specialists.

12. KNOWLEDGE ASSIMILATION/ MANAGEMENT APPLICATION

"Knowledge management" is a buzz word attached to a very real need: The requirement that front-line people have the information they need to be responsive and competitive at the magical "moment of truth." In addition, knowledge makes too many stops without any value being attached to it along the way.

The flood of information besieging the modern organization is like a river at flood crest about to enmesh the surrounding plain. Too much information that does not have the catalyst for conversion into knowledge is as unproductive and stifling as too little information. The ability to help companies gather, analyze, add value to, and—most of all—provide the right information at the right time in the right amount to the right person is invaluable.

We all deal in information. Too few of us deal in knowledge, and fewer still in wisdom. There is a world of opportunity awaiting the transfer of useful and practical knowledge to point-of-action employees and customers.

Action: Organize the basic processes you now use to gather, analyze, and disseminate information for your clients into a learnable, transferable, high-value proposition. You already have the procedure; you simply need to position it correctly.

Example: When a firm's automated voice systems take over 90 percent of the incoming inquiries, the remaining 10 percent doesn't simply go to a reduced staff with the same skills as the old one. These questions are all exceptions, and will require highly skilled respondents with access to varied information sources.

There are certainly more than a dozen new and novel sources of future business acquisition. These are only my candidates to trigger your own think-

How to Acquire Clients

Who Could Make This Up?

Among my more unusual and unexpected clients have been police departments, women's groups, other consulting firms, medical practices, auto dealerships, entrepreneurial start-ups, and trade associations of animal husbandry, fishing, medical devices, tire retreaders, forging, music stores, yacht brokers, and other assorted and sundry groups.

The commonality was only that I was wise enough to respond and recognize how to adapt my basic strengths and generic processes to their situational challenges and specific needs.

My policy is that anyone I can help is a legitimate prospect, and I believe I can help anyone until I'm proved wrong.

—AW

ing. Your business of the future should be more profitable, less wearying, more exciting, less demanding physically, and constantly evolving. Why? Because that's what Ultimate Consultants do.

FROM MY TIME IN THE TRENCHES

The twelve new sources of clients for you to consider:

Source #1: Global Alliances
Source #2: Remote Learning
Source #3: Entrepreneurs
Source #4: Universities and Higher Education
Source #5: The Professions: Medical/Legal/Accounting
Source #6: Mature High-Tech
Source #7: The Retired, The Recreating, The Hobbyist
Source #8: Behavior Modification
Source #9: Life Balance
Source #10: Sales Skills
Source #11: Cultural Accommodation
Source #12: Knowledge Assimilation/Management Application

CHAPTER 10

The Process of Selective Acquisition

How to Reject and Abandon Business in Order to Grow

Many of you will empathize with what I am about to tell you: When I first began in this profession, I wasn't proud. I would accept any business I could. I worked on consulting projects for $5,000, delivered speeches for $750, and gladly sold $10 pamphlets and manuals. I was determined to put bread on the table, and I had only about six months of cash in all the world.

I found to my early happiness that I could stay busy this way, and that elation lasted only as long as it took for me to "grok"[1] the fact that it wasn't important to stay busy—it was important to make a profit. Taking the time to sell and deliver

---

1. A wonderful term for understanding that transcends the English equivalents, from Robert Heinlein, *Stranger in a Strange Land.*

one consulting project a month worth $35,000 was a lot better than $5,000 for one a week. And a single $5,000 speech every other month certainly beat one a week. I'd only have to sell one $120 cassette album to take care of a dozen pamphlet sales.

And, in every case, the *profit* was superior in the larger sale.

The secret to profitable and effective business acquisition is a strategy *not* to accept all business and to be willing to actually *walk away from* certain business. I call this strategy "selective acquisition."

This business is neither about how much you make nor about how much you deliver. It's only about what you *keep*. I know that may sound mercenary, but we can't help others, can't help our family, can't take risks in our profession unless we ensure a healthy profit. Every single week I receive emails and calls from people who inquire about working with me as a coach because, after ten or more years as a consultant, they're still struggling. Anyone who has been in this profession for over a decade and cannot buy what he desires, support the lifestyle she cherishes, and provide for loved ones in the manner he or she seeks is failing.

And that failure is not from insufficient business; it's from *the wrong kind of business.*

THE TEN VERY GOOD REASONS FOR REJECTING PROSPECTIVE BUSINESS

Most of you reading this book have established brands, gained a repute, and have a trove of testimonials, successful experiences, and references that will draw prospects to you. But not every prospect is a good prospect for your practice.

> You have as much obligation as the prospective client to determine whether or not the relationship makes sense for you. You are not a hired hand. You are a potential collaborator. You are entitled to consider your own interests—assuming you truly understand what they are.

Here are the reasons I've found that comprise a template for determining when potential business should be turned down[2] by the consultant.

1. The Requirements Are Too Labor Intensive

Some clients will demand that you be on site at their beck and call. Some organizations have numerous, remote sites, which take forever to visit. There are buyers who require unending reports, summaries, rewrites, and synopses.

The high-value proposition in our profession is to produce dramatic and tangible results that meet the buyer's objectives (improve the client's condition). The low-value proposition is showing up to be a part of the team and an implementer.

2. The Fees Are Too Low

Even veteran consultants tend to look for "door openers" and justify lower fees in return for the dreaded "E" word: Exposure. Accepting low fee work means that you're taking the time away from marketing against high fee work.

I've personally never seen a client who convinces a consultant to take a low initial fee who then says, "You're in! Raise your fees dramatically for the balance of our work together!" Rather, they say, "Okay, let's just keep at our current levels and there shouldn't be a problem, although we'd appreciate a volume discount as we go on."

3. The Work Can Readily Be Delegated

Taking 100 percent of the incorrect work is dumb when you can take 25 to 76 percent of the work and not be involved at all. Personally conducting one hundred interviews or twenty-five focus groups around the country doesn't save you the money of avoiding subcontractors. It costs you the money of tying up all of your available marketing time.

Be willing to accept less of the pie in return for being able to roam around the bakery. Use subcontractors and slightly diminish immediate profit in order to maximize higher long-term profit.

---

2. "Turned down" can mean walking away, referring it to others, subcontracting, or seeking to enlarge the engagement and not accepting it as is.

4. The Work Doesn't Add to Your Learning and, Hence, Your Value

We are paid to learn, which increases our value, which enables us to charge more, which provides still greater learning. This is a wonderful cycle to be caught up in.

Unfortunately, we tend to settle into the "success trap" and continue to do what we've always done, which we could do blindfolded. There is no learning, no growth, and consequently no value enhancement. Turn down, subcontract, or refer business that doesn't help you to grow in some manner.

5. The Buyer Is Problematic

Strange buyers make for terrible clients, because those behaviors don't change just because a proposal has been signed. If a buyer is argumentative, dishonest, unethical, perpetually late, misleading, and/or otherwise unpleasant, don't enter into a collaborative relationship.

Lousy buyers will eat up your time, make unreasonable demands, and fail to honor and respect your legitimate needs. Therefore, they consume inordinate amounts of time that should be spent elsewhere. Just ask anyone who's wasted weeks trying to collect money that should have been easily paid at the outset.

6. There Is Significant Risk

Some projects entail variables you can't influence, people you can't control, and factors you can't anticipate. High-risk projects will drain your energy as you attempt to preserve your reputation and promises.

Although I know some consultants who actually specialize in high-risk (near bankruptcy) turnaround work, any firm that is having trouble paying its bills, or staying out of court, is not a good candidate for fiscal bliss.

"Negative branding" occurs when you are associated with any kind of fiasco in any way. No one gains credit by stating, "Well, if it weren't for me, they would have gone under even faster."

---

7. There May Be an Unsavory Connection with Your Career

Do you really want to work with a firm that downsized 50,000 employees because of poor executive decisions, or with one that polluted the environment and chooses not to own up to its accountability?

You can become "tarred" in working with shady businesses and questionable practices. I wouldn't want to have been a consultant advising human resources on policy and procedure during the headline-grabbing sexual harassment episodes at Astra Pharmaceuticals, for example.

BEST PRACTICES

As a management consultant working mostly in quality, safety, and environmental compliance in the marine industry, my "sales" involve calling on presidents of shipping companies and offering to assist in program implementations, repairs, and audits.

My most effective "sales" technique is to tour the ship(s) and conduct an informal audit/inspection. I bring a camera with me and take pictures of the (sometimes glaring) deficiencies and safety violations. Subsequently, I informally meet with the president and (using the pictures) describe the status of the ships. I also describe the plan of action that I would develop and execute to restore the ships to acceptable standards. Since these people rarely personally tour the ship, it's usually an eyeopener.

—Eugene A. Razzetti, CMC

8. You Will Be Typecast

If you find yourself taking on the same type of business consistently, there's probably a good reason for it: You've become known as a communications expert, or a workshop leader, or a facilitator, or a mergers authority. That's fine if you want to specialize, but specialization does not lead to maximum profitability.

Your goal should be to stay "light on your feet" so that you can adjust to changes in the economy, technology, society, and business ethos. Reject business that further and further paints you into a narrow corner of the profession.

9. There Are No Clear Objectives or Metrics

As a successful and reputable practitioner, some buyers will approach you with a fait accompli, asking you to help out in a vague area or a nebulous fashion. This often appears to be "found money," since there was no marketing and there is no arguing over fees.

But if there are no clear goals and no measures of progress, you've been paid to enter the La Brea Tar Pits and the next sight you see is likely to be a saber-toothed tiger at about five hundred feet underground. What seems like "easy money" rarely is.

10. You Just Don't Like the Smell, Sound, or Feel of It

Go with your gut. There are people and environments that will give you very bad vibes. Your gut instinct at this stage of your career is an awfully good bet. If you don't like it, don't do it.

Consultants are sometimes hired to be the scapegoat, the public enemy, and the executive excuse. There are no objectives involved other than that. No matter how much you're being paid, who needs such grief, hostility, and stress? That is not the road to becoming the Ultimate Consultant.

> Every piece of unpleasant business will affect your ability to manage good business. At this stage of your career, there's no reason for accepting this as a "necessary evil." Eschew bad business, now and forever.

Turning down prospective business is relatively simple, although you may have to bite on a bullet or take a strong drink. But it's child's play compared to ending existing business.

THE FIVE VERY GOOD REASONS FOR PULLING THE PLUG ON EXISTING BUSINESS

This is the area that drives most consultants to rend their garments—how can you give up business you took so long to find, worked so hard to close, and whose money clears the bank?! It's not difficult, because hanging on to too much "stuff" just creates drag, friction, and fatigue.

In addition to the ten reasons above, most of which can be applied to existing business as well, here are five more reasons to cut the cord, pull the plug, and say "Ciao."

1. Business That Is Barely Profitable

This seems like a no-brainer, but we tend to keep business out of loyalty, inertia, and sloth. This is stuff that has been around since we originally needed to put bread on the table, and we're reluctant to abandon the security blanket.

The point, of course, is that we've never raised prices and can no longer reasonably do so. These have become friendships rather than client relationships, and who raises prices on a friend? Refer this business to someone else who needs the work and who will, ironically, probably pay it more attention and do a better job. It doesn't mean you're a bad person.

2. Clients Who Provide No Upside Potential

You want as clients large firms with a surfeit of lateral potential. Or if you work with smaller firms, then you need a coherent, finite project. If the firm's size, finances, or prospects seem to prohibit expansion business, then don't take on minor projects after your initial foray.

Don't hang around doing "busy work" or small time stuff. Worse than the image and the small payment, it's a tremendous time waster. No, it's not better than doing "nothing" if "nothing" can be construed as sitting around planning about how you're going to penetrate Microsoft or Sony.

3. You're Repeating Yourself

If you're giving workshops to the same people on slightly different subjects (or you find yourself straining to create new material), you're coaching the same executives on different (barely) issues, or you're so familiar that the employees simply consider you a part of the management team, it's time to leave.

These are usually "make work" assignments that the buyer and you conjure up to perpetuate the relationship. Instead of making work, you should make yourself scarce.

4. Client Conditions Significantly Change

We've all been in the midst of consulting nirvana when our buyer is transferred, the budgets are cut, the competition steals the thunder, or the basic premises prove invalid. It may be time to cut and run.

I don't mean that you leave the client in the lurch, but I do suggest that you approach the buyer to point out that the original objectives are no longer relevant or possible to achieve. (You can't increase sales when six top people are recruited away and take their customers with them.) Work out a financial settlement, if needed, but don't try to make the goat fly. You will just have an unhappy goat.

5. Your Conditions (Strategies) Significantly Change

Many consultants change their strategy in line with changing times. But they are weighed down by the mass of the existing client base, which they can't bring themselves to jettison. New strategies (and include in here new life style goals and personal expectations) require new client configurations.

No matter what you're being paid, you can't spend more time with the family if you retain clients who demand excessive travel. No matter what the fee, you won't become known as a strategist if your client base inadvertently builds your brand as that of human resources consultant. No matter how lucrative the deal, you won't be able to work on business growth if you're locked into the IT department.

Like the kid trying to cross the "monkey bars" in the playground, you don't make headway by holding on with two hands to the position you currently occupy. You must, counterintuitively, let go with one hand if you are to reach out and advance your position.

It's difficult to shed a client—a butterfly's metamorphosis is a day at the beach in comparison. The latter is genetically engineered and the former scrapes and claws against every tenet we've been raised to believe. But it's important to do so if you want to acquire dramatic, high-profit, and expansionary business.

You can't reach out until you let go.

MANAGING NEW BUSINESS POTENTIAL AND PROFIT

"Selective acquisition" also means taking on business on your terms. We compromise far too much in this profession. No patient, to my knowledge, asks a doctor to negotiate fees.[3] Lawyers, or at least good ones, don't accept client fee resistance. Universities, by and large, suggest that you get a loan, earn a scholarship, or work at a job, but the tuition is the tuition and it must be paid from some source.

We allow ourselves to be intimidated, bullied, cajoled, lured, and otherwise compromised by the siren song of the buyer dangling a piece of business before our eyes. I don't know about you, but I'm not a carp and I can't breathe underwater. Take away my oxygen—my profits—and I die.

The Twilight Zone

This situation occurred when I was a less experienced salesperson (still selling outplacement services). I had an appointment with the HR person at Remington Products. The individual I was supposed to meet was delayed for about forty-five minutes. While I sat patiently in the lobby, I watched five salespeople come into the lobby and ask to see the decision maker/buyer for his or her particular product or service.

Each time the person came out and asked the salesperson to "make your pitch" right there on the spot! I listened to people try to sell temporary services, copiers, manufacturing parts, and several other products. None of them managed to get another meeting or make a sale. By this time I was quaking in my shoes. The HR director with whom I was scheduled to meet finally came out and, much to my relief, walked me back to his office! Phew!

—Julie Jansen, Julie Jansen LLC

---

3. Yes, I know that HMOs and insurers might, but that's because the medical profession has never adopted an intelligent billing system, and a change in economic and business conditions pulled the rug out from under it.

Successful consultants should be in a position to do more than merely pursue business and try to land it. They should be pursuing business and *accepting it on their own terms.* What if the buyer has his or her own terms? You don't understand: The buyer's terms revolve around the output side—the value of the improvement delivered with your assistance. The terms you seek are on the input side—the fees to be paid, in what manner, on what dates, and with what margins for you.

The notion of managing new business (If it's old business, it's already too late; if you didn't do it right the first time, it's money left on the table) and its resultant profitability should be no more alien to you than managing a project to ensure it finishes on time with the results delivered. Why is it we're so enamored with client project management and so indifferent to our own fiscal management?

Here are some areas to be vigilant in if you are to acquire the right clients, with the right terms, at the right times.

Fee Amount. Always offer the client options with increased value propositions and escalating fees.[4] It's not the purpose of this book to discuss fee setting per se, but you must be willing to charge a strong return on investment (ROI) quotient. In other words, if you're providing the client with $5 million of savings on an annualized basis, just 3 percent of the *first year savings alone* is $150,000. If you're providing a $1 million executive in a $400 million dollar company with a better team of direct reports, isn't that worth, say, 5 percent of the annual gross ($200,000) or 10 percent of his salary ($100,000)?

> You can wrench your arm out of joint by patting yourself on the back and congratulating the person in the mirror on the "big hit." You're better off using that arm to guide your hand to sharpen your pencil and ensure that the "big hit" becomes "big profit" right at the outset.

---

4. See the third book in this Jossey-Bass/Pfeiffer series: *Value-Based Fees: How to Charge—and Get—What You're Worth* (2002).

Payment Intervals. Offer discounts for full payment upon commencement. Short of that, condense the elapsed time in which payments take place. For example, even though the project may be expected to last nine months, there is nothing wrong with asking for 50 percent on acceptance and 50 percent in 60 days. What's the worse that can happen? You'll usually compromise on 50 percent on acceptance and 50 percent in 90 days, still better than waiting for nine months.

Accountabilities and "Fail Safe." Specify clearly what your client's (buyer's) responsibilities are, what yours are, and what you share jointly. For example, include a clear statement in your proposal that either of you will immediately notify the other of any new development or information gathered that significantly impacts the scope or progress of the project. The client must tell you if a proposed divestiture or acquisition, for instance, has arisen that imperils morale, hiring, resource allocation, and so on. You must tell the client if you learn by chance that three top performers are interviewing with a competitor.[5]

Internal Logistical Support and a "Virtual Team." While I don't pose as a prima donna, I do request of the client that certain provisions be made that would be offered to any visiting professional colleague. I ask for a private office or cubicle when I'm onsite; for a phone that can accommodate my computer modem; for "light" secretarial support (scheduling interviews, providing conference rooms, typing up an agenda); and proper identification for unescorted movement through the facility and between floors. These modest, approved support mechanisms will save you time and expenses right from the outset.

Missed Payment Deadlines. If your fee is being paid on a scheduled basis, and/or if expense payments are due, do not allow long "grace" periods. Often these payments are sitting on someone's desk who is on vacation or overburdened with "higher priority" work. (I recently found that an overdue check had

---

5. You might want to consider this policy: Whenever anyone approaches me in a client organization and asks if I can be told something in confidence, I always reply, "Only if you understand that if what you tell me significantly affects my client's well-being—and I will be the sole judge of that—then I cannot maintain your confidence." This provides you with the ethical basis to divulge what you learn if necessary.

never been issued because a temporary secretary had responded to an inquiry from accounts payable by telling them that I had already been paid, so they cancelled the requisition!) On your invoices, note that all fees and reimbursements are due on receipt, not at 30 days, net or even less. In that manner, if you do choose to allow a thirty-day grace period, the clock can start from your invoice date and not thirty days thereafter. When cash you are due is not in your bank account, you are losing money.

Consider the following additional subtleties to accelerate payments:

Include your federal tax ID number on all invoices and statements so that accounts payable does not have to take the time to request it

Include a self-addressed, stamped envelope or a FedEx air bill with your account number and request it be used for the check conveyance

Find a contact in accounts payable who supports your client's department and send bills to that person by name with a cover note

Send an email version of the bill with hard copy to follow; this sometimes starts the payment process faster

Keep copies of all receipts submitted for expense reimbursement so that, if the originals are misplaced, you can quickly supply replacements

---

The manner in which you manage a client relationship at the outset will establish the tone for the long-term relationship. Be fair, but be firm. Don't forget, this is a peer-level partnership.

Provide clear explanation of any unusual items on expense reimbursements, for example, if you travel first class but bill for coach, or if you used limos because taxis were unavailable or unreliable, so that there is no need for a series of questions and responses about individual items

When appropriate, simply build in expenses and include them in your fee, so that numerous invoices are unnecessary[6]

6. The clearer your objectives and project scope, the easier it is to make intelligent estimates of expense projections. Even if you somewhat underestimate, it will be offset by your ability to collect your money more quickly (within the fee schedule) and not have to document and wait for reimbursement.

"Selective acquisition" includes the establishment of policies and under-standings that will enable you to maximally perform your job as well as speed payments and maximize profits.

THE MERCEDES-BENZ SYNDROME

The most fascinating aspect of selective acquisition for me has been my gradual comprehension of how much people expect to get what they pay for. This is as applicable in the business realm and in the selection of consultants as it is any-where.

When someone purchases an $80,000 Mercedes-Benz, they expect it to be built well, engineered excellently, and to be a superb performing car. *The inter-esting aspect of this expectation, however, is that the buyer will actually work hard to realize those expectations.* In some models, the Daimler-Benz engineers dictated that the seat warmers would automatically turn themselves down or off as a safety feature, irrespective of the fact that the driver might want the seat heated for lengthy amounts of time. (Other cars permit indefinite warming.) It's annoy-ing to have the seat turn itself to a lower setting on a cold winter morning after a few minutes of driving, but the owners would generally shrug and consider it to be a legitimate safety feature.

For years, Mercedes obstinately refused to install cup holders or a tele-scoping steering wheel. Again, well-heeled customers in love with the status and cachet of a Mercedes brushed off the intransigence as a design or safety concession. Mercedes drivers will tend to say, "This is a rough road," while drivers of lesser cars might comment, "I'm unhappy with the car's suspension."

Here is the most efficacious way for veteran, successful consultants to raise fees. It's complex, and you might want to turn down a corner of this page for easy future reference: If you want to raise fees, raise fees. At this point in your career, the world is reversed and value follows fees.

People believe they get what they pay for, and they'll actually contort logic and scramble for explanations to justify and rationalize that position. If someone saw Sir Laurence Olivier in a bad performance, they were much more likely to believe the writing, directing, supporting cast, lighting, or sound systems were to blame—and not the great actor. Can beluga caviar or Lafite Rothschild wine possibly not taste excellent? You'd better clean your palate, because it can't be the product!

This same incredible human behavior holds true in consulting. Once you are successfully divorced from the hired hand and implementer roles and you're truly viewed as a valued counselor and advisor (you're the Rand think tank and not an Ace Hardware Store), your value will actually increase as your fee increases. That's right: Fees don't follow value, but value follows fees that you ascend to certain exalted and rarified Ultimate Consultant heights.

In acquiring clients, selective acquisition dictates the following:

1. Fewer clients at higher per client fees are superior to many clients at lower per client fees. (Even if the gross billings are the same, profitability is much higher in the first instance.)
2. Attracting fewer, more lucrative clients is easier at a point in one's career when brand recognition, successful experiences, and strong testimonials and endorsements have been created.
3. "Raising fees" means that you can charge a higher percentage of the overall value being delivered to the client and the client will still believe that the return on investment is excellent. This is not about fee schedules or time-based billing rates.[7]
4. This cycle is reinforcing. As you charge higher rates based on your repute and/or brand, you will become more confident; you will become more in demand; and you will feel upward pressure to raise fees still further.

---

7. Simply stated, this would mean that a recognized and admired consultant can assess a fee of, say, $250,000 to help in generating a projected $5 million in savings, whereas a newer or unknown consultant might only be able to command $100,000 for the same effort. With subjective and anecdotal measures (for example, team building, image, safety, reliability) the disparity is even greater.

The One That Got Away

Something that has the potential to sneak up and snatch a sale at just about any time is the crossing of the line between confidence and cockiness. It can happen to anyone and usually happens when business is going very well.

I remember telling my wife, after a meeting with a prospect, "If I don't get this client or it takes a while for him to sign on, it's because I rushed the process." I knew I went too fast, from introduction to proposal.

I went too fast on the first two of the following three steps:

- Ask all the questions (really probe)
- Make them hurt
- Demonstrate my ability to be the solution

Why did I do this? I think it was because I was "on top of the world." Business was very good and growing. I was having a hard time making my way through the list of referrals on my desk, and my subconscious assumed this prospect was meeting with me because he was ready to buy.

I feel fortunate that I recognized it immediately. It is now one of my forefront issues before every meeting. It taught me to put together an (internal) agenda for every meeting. I now know exactly what information I want to get from each prospect, and I make sure I get it. I know exactly what I want to say to determine the prospect's true wants and needs.

—John Martinka, President, Business Resource Group, Inc.

The Mercedes-Benz Syndrome creates an upward draft because buyers will believe that you're good and will, as Mercedes drivers, dismiss or rationalize perceived "flaws." You will engender far greater benefit of the doubt. Your positions and conjecture will be accepted more readily. Your risks will be viewed as more prudent. Your methodology will meet less resistance.

To fully exploit the Mercedes-Benz Syndrome so that your business acquisition process can be as targeted and efficient as possible, consider the following tactics:

Burnish Your Public Image. Your website, materials, press kit, products, and other public, tangible manifestations of "who you are" have to be absolutely first rate. The case has to be cleaned and polished. Too many successful consultants allow their websites and collateral materials to become obsolete and faded.

> The client is the one afflicted with the Mercedes-Benz Syndrome, but the consultant is the one who is the carrier.

Lead with Your Most Powerful Engine. Prominently display and promote your successful engagements, testimonial letters, and endorsements. Within non-disclosure constraints, publicize your client list. Wealthy and successful people buy only the best. Well-run and successful companies do the same. Successful people like to be around similarly successful people. Provide a test drive and demonstrate what the car is capable of doing.

Create and Sustain the Cachet. Create, nurture, and extend your "brands" to the maximum extent.[8] When CEOs, desperate for strategy help, yell, "Get McKinsey," they aren't concerned about price, competitive quotes, or the McKinsey methodology. What they want is that brand in the door as soon as possible. Auto companies create strategic brand advertising. Consultants must create strategic brand awareness through publishing, speaking, interviews, word-of-mouth, and other "campaign" alternatives.

   If prospective buyers perceive that you are the "Mercedes of the business," then you will have short-cut the early part of the credibility and relationship building processes and will have obviated the need for any fee discussions. When someone says, "Get me Alan Weiss," then my value has already been accepted and my suggestions—even if seemingly bizarre or counterintuitive—will be supported. The only thing left to decide is just how high my fee should be.

---

8. See the second book in The Ultimate Consultant series from Jossey-Bass/Pfeiffer: *How to Establish a Unique Brand in the Consulting Profession* (2001).

Even during economic downturns, the high-end luxury car market thrives. The top-of-the-line Mercedes, Ferraris, and Aston Martins will sell out their production runs. Top-of-the-line consultants—whom I've been calling "Ultimate Consultants"—will similarly thrive, because high-end buyers will insist on believing that they will get what they pay for.

It's up to us not to let them down.

FROM MY TIME IN THE TRENCHES: CHAPTER 10

Not all business is good business, and this becomes *increasing true as a consultant becomes more successful.* The process of selective acquisition calls for the consultant to deliberately avoid certain type of business (poor profitability, high risk, low learning, unpleasant buyer) and to target those that offer maximum growth and profit. This applies also to existing business. If one has to "let go in order to reach out," then existing business must also be culled if it does not fit into the optimal profile for the consultant's best interests.

Longevity is not a sufficient reason to maintain a client relationship. Ironically, the probability is high that you are also not servicing such clients in their best interest either.

Managing new business potential is another selective process wherein we are able to maximize profit through efficiency and expense reduction, while pursuing long-term client relationships under conditions best for our own long-term interests as well. Many consultants relax their guard and sacrifice the power of their initial sale by allowing relationships and working conditions to default to a non-peer-level relationship. In other words, the Rand Corporation delivers a plumber.

The Mercedes-Benz Syndrome states that buyers expect to get what they pay for. Hence, and in an almost Alice-in-the-Looking-Glass world, at some stage in our careers value begins to follow fee rather than the traditional converse. So while high value generated higher fees for us to sustain our growth, at a certain critical juncture our rising fees justify higher expected value in the eyes of the buyer. This is a branding or repute phenomenon which occurs in almost every highly successful career, but which is often missed.

> The primary fuel for selective acquisition is the bizarre but true fact that, at a given critical juncture in one's success trajectory, value will follow fee rather than fee following value. When that occurs, business acquisition becomes both easier than ever and more lucrative than ever *if one understands the nature and application of the phenomenon.*

FROM MY TIME IN THE TRENCHES: THE BOOK

We create our own targets of opportunity, ideally based on market need that exists or that we create; on competencies we possess or can develop; and on passions which drive us. The generalist has more opportunities, per force, than the specialist. However, either can create specialized and customized "attacks" on high-profile targets of opportunity.

The ideal acquisition posture occurs when prospects approach you, improving the psychology and dynamic of the sale. But successful consultants, more so than neophytes and average practitioners, are able to attack, flank, and/or infiltrate a target account, because they have the resources, time, and experience to do so.

Relationship building is largely about understanding human behavior and seeking to influence it. Subtleties and nuance are more powerful than brute force, so that gentle techniques such as controlling a discussion, finding emotional triggers, and empathic listening become important competencies. However, it is equally important to take a hard stand against unacceptable behaviors and unappealing prospects.

We've heard every objection under the sun. In a macro sense, they all are about "no hurry," "no time," "no money," and/or "no trust." All can be readily countered, particularly by using the knowledge of the common objections to visualize the future and prepare the proper response. The client's own momentum can be reversed and used in our favor through techniques such as turnaround questions and direct challenges.

Unlike objections, which can be forecast, there are current and new busi-

Who Could Make This Up?

I worked for Calgon (the specialty water treatment company) for five years on an annual six-figure retainer renewable each year. I helped them when they were owned by Merck, assisted in their sale to English China Clay, and helped them as a component of that new owner.

At the conclusion of the fourth year, as was our habit, I sat down with the CEO to determine our goals for the following year. At the conclusion of the meeting I said, as I had each year before, "Are the same arrangements acceptable?"

"No," said the CEO, "not this time."

I was aghast, having thought all was well. After all, I wasn't raising the retainer, only asking for the identical arrangements as each year prior, which I thought were equitable.

"This time," said the CEO, "raise the amount, because we're not paying you what you're worth to us." The amount was a 30 percent increase in my retainer fee.

As far as I can recall, that was the last time I was ever speechless in front of a client.

—AW

ness acquisition sources we must constantly monitor and mine in order to ensure as eclectic and comprehensive a prospect pipeline as possible.

The business is about influencing a buyer, and a buyer is someone who can produce a check on his or her own volition. Committees are never buyers. You can, however, build critical mass and momentum among key advisors. Providing value early and for free is an intelligent strategy. "You have to give to get."

Since the marketplace for consulting services is finite, growth will usually take place at someone else's expense. Even "locked in" relationships can be breeched. Sometimes it's a matter of maintaining high visibility while waiting for the appropriate opportunity or for someone else's bad news. "Low hanging fruit," however, is a relatively easy approach to gaining immediate increased market share from others.

> The more successful you are for the longer time, the easier it is to acquire both the wrong kind of business *and* the right kind of business. Why settle for the former when you can select the latter?

The most economical "new" business is repeat business. "Thinking of the fourth sale first" means considering a client relationship as an organic and long-lived process, not as a finite project or "event." Trust is best developed through intelligent "pushback" rather than mindless acquiescence and avoidance of problems. The best tactic to fight back against those trying to steal your own market share is the "discount principle" of making yourself virtually prohibitively expensive to replace by any other source.

Finally, selective acquisition requires that you reject inappropriate business, cull poor performing existing business, manage new accounts rigorously from the outset to maximize profit, and understand that people believe they get what they pay for.

Consequently, at some point that you must be able to discern for yourself, your value will actually follow your fees as you escalate them. And that is the ultimate position for the Ultimate Consultant.

Index

titles which are not, 26; knowing name of, 21–22; locating different organization, 122; maximizing sale when approached by, 32–34; never abandon, 140; objections raised by, 54–69; problematic, 166; questions to help identify, 22; as real client, 133; searching for real need of, 132; techniques for direct interaction with, 25–27; unacceptable behaviors by, 50–51. *See also* Organizations; Relationship building

Emotional priority questions, 50

Emotional targeting, 48–50

Emotional triggers, 136

Employees: building friendship relationship with, 30; cultural accommodation of, 159–160. *See also* Organizations

Encyclopaedia Britannica, 75

Endorsement, 88

Entrepreneurs, 149–150

Ernst & Young, 42

The Executive Techniques, 150

Expressive behavior types: compared to other types, 40–41; described, 39*fig*, 40; objections correlated with, 58*fig*

F

Feasibility buyer, defining, 26

Federal Reserve Bank of New York, 129

FedEx, 9

Fenno, B., 121

Fishing expeditions, 104–105

Flanking maneuver strategy, 25–27

Fleet Bank, 145

Flexibility, 141

Fortune poll, 130

"Fourth sale" metaphor, 128–130, 143

Fox, H., 22

Franchising, 83

"Free" help, 92–94

Friedman, N., 84

Frontal attack strategy, 20–21

G

GE (General Electric), 129

General Motors, 150

Global alliances, 147

Global vacations, 79–81

H

Hamacher, D., 5, 154

Hasbro, 75

Hewlett-Packard, 21, 29, 42, 74n.1, 75, 94, 152, 156

High visibility creation, 114–117

Honest Selling Breakfast Club, 8

HR (Human resources) departments, 102–103

The Hunt for Red October (Clancy), 88

I

IBM, 3, 145, 153

Infiltrating trade associations, 86–87

Infiltration strategy, 27–31

Insanity, 59

Institute for Business Renewal, 29

Internal logistical support, 173

Internet: "reversed flow" use, 75–76; visibility by publishing on the, 114–115, 119

J

Jansen, J., 171

Jeff Magee International, Inc., 116

Julie Jansen LLC, 171

K

Kaiser Permanente, 136

Keynote speaking, 80, 115, 122

"Kick over the table" strategy, 106

Kinko's, 85

Knowledge assimilation, 160–161

"Knowledge management," 160

L

Legal clients, 151–152

Levi Strauss, 156

Life balance, 156–157

Listening strategy, 45–46, 47

"Low hanging fruit" organizations, 111–114

M

Magee, J. L., 116

Management application, 160–161

Mapes, H., 89

Marine Midland Bank, 29, 145

Market need: convergence of competency, passion and, 3*fig*; necessary to successful selling, 2–3; organization acceptance of, 113; searching for the real, 132

Market share: creating high visibility to increase, 114–117; harvesting "low hanging fruit" to increase, 111–114; moving into vacated consulting space and, 117–118; need to expand, 109–111; reflections on trespassing strategies for, 125–126; success traps from lack of growth in, 110*fig*; techniques for trespassing on others's, 120–125; value campaign to increase, 118–120

Marketing: "cold call" viability criteria for, 12–13; creating high visibility, 114–117; as creation of need among buyers, 3n.1; customizing assaults during, 12–14; hypothetical approach to the *New York Times*, 14–16; impact of generalizing vs. specializing on, 7, 10–11; "low hanging fruit" harvesting, 111–114; Mercedes-Benz Syndrome applied to, 178–179; to prospective clients, 92–108; trespassing strategies, 120–127; value campaign compared to traditional, 120. *See also* Client acquisition avenues; Selling

Martinka, J., 177

Martiny, M., 74n.1

Mass loyalty creation, 141

McDonald's, 3, 121

McKinsey, 3, 85, 178

McNaughton, D., 132

The McNaughton Group, Inc., 132

Medical clients, 151–152

Mercedes-Benz, 94, 145

Mercedes-Benz Syndrome: applied to brand development, 178–179; applied to selective client acquisition, 175–177, 180; reflections on, 179

Merck, 14, 21, 29, 32, 75, 94, 129–130, 145, 181

Merck, G., 5

Merrill, D., 37

Micallef, J., 77

Michelin North America, 93

Michigan Bell, 98

"Middle man" strategy, 76–77

Miller, A., 57

Miller, N., 142

Min/max meeting objections, 44

Motorola, 152

MultiTrack Sales Consulting, 22

N

National Fisheries Institute, 115

Negative branding, 166

Networking, 86. *See also* Relationships

New business. *See* Client acquisition

New direction strategy, 122

New York Times, 14–16, 145

Newsletters, 119

NH (no hurry) objections: consultant response to, 62–63; described, 55, 56; indicators of, 62; indicators of successful overcoming of, 63

NM (no money) objections: consultant response to, 64; described, 55, 56; indicators of, 63–64; indicators of successful overcoming of, 64

NN (no need) objections: consultant response to, 59; described, 55, 56; indicators of, 59; indicators of successful overcoming of, 60

Normative pressure technique, 92

NT (no trust) objections: consultant response to, 61; described, 55, 56; indicators of, 60; indicators of successful overcoming of, 61

NYNEX, 98

O

Objections: dealing with "blind spot," 54–55; four major areas of, 55–57; rebutting arguments for basic areas of, 57–65; reflections on, 69; sample rebuttals and, 66–69; visualizing the future preparation for, 65–66

Objectives: conflicting and/or unreasonable, 51; establishing buyer, 45; establishing min/max meeting, 44; rejecting client without clear, 168; scope creep outside of, 106–107, 140. *See also* Economic buyers

Olivier, Sir L., 176

Op-ed newspaper articles, 81

Options: preparing alternative, 65; providing client with, 33; providing one above the budget, 33; pushback tactic challenging immediate, 135

Organizations: budgets of, 33; building relationships with employees of, 30; conducting informal audit/inspection of, 167; creating mass loyalty within, 141; cultural differences within, 159–160; internal logistical support/virtual team in, 173; internal politics of, 104; knowledge assimilation/management application by, 160–161; locating different buyer within, 122; "low hanging fruit," 111–114; market need acceptance by, 113; publishing strategies including target, 119. *See also* Clients; Economic buyers; Employees

P

PACER Associates, Inc., 31, 136, 149

Parachuting strategy, 122–123

Passion: described, 5; three trajectories of consultant, 6*fig*

Payment intervals, 173

Payments: managing intervals of, 173; missed deadlines for, 173–174

Peat Marwick, 146

Personal networking, 86. *See also* Relationships

Poole, B., 158

Poole Resources, Inc., 158

Poor chemistry, 51

Power sales technique, 92

Practical Computer Solutions, 17

Preparing alternatives, 65

Preparing analysis, 66

SB (stumbling blocks): described, 95; strategies for handling, 96–97
Scanlon, J., 39
Scope creep, 106–107, 140
Selective client acquisition: importance of profit and, 163–164, 175; Mercedes-Benz Syndrome applied to, 176–179, 180; reasons for rejecting clients and, 164–168. *See also* Client acquisition
Selling: conditions essential to successful, 2–7; developing skills for, 157; false assumptions and, 158; frontal attack strategy for, 20–21; importance of economic buyer to, 21–27; informal audit/inspection technique used for, 167; maximizing when approached by buyer, 32–34; to meet buyer need, 3n.1; next project during current one, 141; trust as requirement for, 20; truth as ally for, 47; using emotional triggers for, 136; "walking away" from, 33. *See also* Marketing
"Selling myself," 131
Seminar workshops, 115–116, 122–123
Serendipity, 30
Serino, P., 113
"Six degrees of separation" approach, 88, 119–120
Sobel, A., 29
Social contacts, 30–31
"Sole source" supplier, 100–101
"Specialize or die" rubric, 7
Sponsor leverage strategy, 123
Stanford Transportation Group, 62
State Street Bank, 138
Steig, D., 17
Steinberg, L., 47
Stumbling blocks (SB), 95, 96–97
"Success trap," 13
Summit Consulting Group, Inc., 19
Summit Resource Catalog, 76
Suppliers: selling to your client's, 85–86; "sole source," 100–101
Synergistic alliances, 115–117

T

Targets of opportunity: creating specific, 14; low volume/high focus approach to, 17; strategies for hitting new, 14–16
Taylor, B., 124
The Taylor Company, 124
Teaching activities, 29
Teague, J., 7n.4
The Telephone Doctor, 84
Testimonials, 15n.6

Texaco, 145
Texas Instruments, 152–153
Thomas, D., 144
Thomson, M., 103
Thomson Management Solutions, Inc., 103
"Threat" factors: described, 101–102; dwindling funds, 105–106; fishing expeditions, 104–105; human resources, 102–103; prevailing politics, 104; scope creep, 106–107, 140; unions, 102
365 Sales Tips for Winning Business (Miller), 57
Time magazine, 19
Times Mirror, 145
Times-Mirror Group, 75
"Timing" issues, 63. *See also* NH (no hurry) objections
Trade associations: leadership of, 119; networking through affiliation with, 86–87; potential clients through, 123
Trespassing marketing strategies: belie the fad, 124–125; using different direction, 122; finding different economic buyer, 122; leverage through sponsor, 123; parachute in, 122–123; reflections on using, 125–127; using, 120–122
"True buyer," 21
Trust: developed through pushback, 133–138; mutual respect basis of, 137; objections regarding lack of, 55; pursuing additional projects and, 141; required for selling, 20; taking time to build relationship, 131. *See also* NT (no trust) objections
Truth, 47
Turnaround questioning, 46

U

Unacceptable behaviors, 50–51
Unions, 102
University clients, 150–151
University of Georgia, 29
University of Illinois, 29
University of Phoenix, 147
University of Rhode Island, 29
"Unpromotional" article publishing, 78
Unreasonable objectives, 51

V

V (vetoes): described, 95; strategies for handling, 96–97
Vacations, 79–81
Value campaign, 118–120
Vetoes (V), 95, 96–97
Visibility creation, 114–117
Visualizing the future preparation, 65–66

W

Wagner, G. E., 8
"Walking away," 33
The Wall Street Journal, 19
Website marketing strategies, 8. *See also*
 Internet
White paper, 28

"Woo-woo" effect, 65
Workshops, 115–116, 122–123
Writing a book, 88–89

Z

Zemke, R., 65
Zintz, A. C., 60, 86

Printed in the United States
96106LV00004B/33-52/A

9 780787 955144